6.75

INSURING
YOUR HOME

INSURING YOUR HOME

Stephen Mink

CONGDON & WEED, INC.
New York

Copyright © 1984 by Stephen Mink

Library of Congress Cataloging in Publication Data

Mink, Stephen.
Insuring your home.

Includes index.
1. Insurance, Homeowners. I. Title
HG9986.M56   1984   368'.096   84-9453
ISBN 0-86553-134-X
ISBN 0-312-92334-1 (St. Martin's Press)

Published by Congdon & Weed, Inc.
298 Fifth Avenue, New York, N.Y. 10001

Distributed by St. Martin's Press
175 Fifth Avenue, New York, N.Y. 10010

Published simultaneously in Canada by Methuen Publications
2330 Midland Avenue, Agincourt, Ontario M1S 1P7

Contents

Contents

12. Knowing Your Rights 178

*Policy Interpretation • Established Policy
Interpretations • Fluctuating Interpretations • Third Party
Negligence • Proximate Cause and Concurrent Causation
Theory • Appraisal and Suit • Subrogation • Unfair
Claim Settlement Practices Acts • Fair
Treatment • Salvage • Statements • Nonwaiver
Agreements • Reservation of Rights Letters • Cancellation*

Index 205

Introduction

WHEN I first began working as an insurance adjuster years ago, I was constantly amazed at how little policyholders knew about their homeowners insurance. Time and time again, I saw how such a lack of knowledge leads to financial loss and to needless heartbreak as well. I also discovered that there was no easy-to-understand guide available to consumers on the subject of homeowners insurance, and after many years of working in the insurance industry, I decided to put together that essential guide.

This book is the result of months of research as well as many conversations with people involved in all aspects of insurance work. The purpose of the book is to introduce you to the vast subject of homeowners insurance—I will point out how to shop for the right policy for yourself, take you through the basic coverages and provisions that apply to homeowners policies, and then describe the procedures involved in filing a claim.

It would be impossible to write a book of this type that would be equally true and correct in all states. To address each variation of policy coverages, claims handling practices, and statute and case law applicable in every state would be a monumental task, and the end product would be totally unreadable to all but the highly dedicated or the certifiably insane. In some states, court precedents and industry practice will be well established on a particular question, while in other states the decisions on the same question may vary widely. There are principles that are universally accepted by the insurance industry on a national basis (although they could change tomorrow), and some that vary from state to state. Therefore some of the statements made in this book will be more accurate in one state than in another.

There are a handful of people who deserve my sincerest thanks for their hard work, support, feedback, criticism, and assistance on this project: Lea Guyer Gordon at Congdon & Weed for her valuable input and hours of work editing this manuscript; Carol Shrum for her effort in deciphering my rough drafts and typing this book; and my father, Earl Mink, for his advice and support. Thanks also to George Guinane, C.P.C.U., in Bloomington, Illinois, Tom Manor at the G.A.B. National Education Center at Aurora, Colorado, Dominick Yezzi at the Insurance Services Office in New York, the staff at the Insurance Information Institute in San Francisco, Jorge Sandovel at the California Department of Insurance office, and Dorothy Wolfe for their consultation and technical assistance. In acknowledgment of the fact that professional growth occurs largely through the efforts of those who serve as teachers in one form or another, I would like to thank the many individuals whom I have worked for and with over the years, who have taken the time to share with me their considerable knowledge and expertise.

Stephen Mink
Berkeley, California

1 Understanding Insurance

- *Purpose of Insurance* • *Being Knowledgeable*
  About Claims • *Common Sense*

YOU turn the car into the driveway and see the charred remains of roof rafters through the scattered black shingles. Smoke-tinted windows have been broken out by firemen, the paint above them gray with soot. Inside, thin layers of black ash peel from the walls and ceilings. Loosened floor tiles float about in puddles, and warped floorboards buckle under saturated carpets. From room to blackened room you walk, stepping through the debris, breathing the putrid odor of heavy smoke.

It sounds like a dark and distant nightmare. Yet every day, approximately two thousand homes are damaged by fire in the United States. And fire is just one form of calamity resulting in the loss of real and personal property. The awesome damages caused by wind are evident after the passing of each hurricane or tornado. Recently, a devastating tornado swept through the Carolinas, leaving hundreds homeless. A ruptured plumbing fixture can result in damages amounting to thousands

1

of dollars. Or it may be burglary, vandalism, a misguided vehicle, or a smoldering frying pan. The kinds of perils to which your property is exposed is limited only by the extreme confines of physical reality and Murphy's Law.

It is hoped that most people will not have to experience a tragic fire, flood, or hurricane to underscore the need of not only having a comprehensive homeowners insurance policy but also of having a policy that is tailored to their individual specific needs.

The purpose of this guide to homeowners insurance is twofold: (1) to help you understand and select the right coverage for your requirements; and (2) to guide you in filing a claim should some damage occur to your property and to explain how reimbursement works.

Purpose of Insurance

Homeowners insurance was created to provide protection for your most basic and treasured assets—your home and personal belongings. A lack of knowledge about the conditions of the policy you select substantially reduces the value of your insurance protection. In other words, the value of your policy increases in proportion to your ability to use it effectively. In order to utilize the policy most effectively, you must develop a complete and thorough understanding of the nature of your homeowners policy and of insurance in general.

To derive the full benefit from your homeowners insurance, you must become familiar with the coverage provided by the policy. The more you know about coverage, the less likely you will be to overlook potentially covered losses or to file claims for losses that are not covered, which may adversely affect your claim record. You will also be in a position to recognize your potential exposures and to purchase your insurance accordingly. For example, an acquaintance of mine who lives in Arizona lost hundreds of dollars worth of frozen food during a power outage. After learning, to his dismay, that the loss was not covered under his homeowners policy, he bought a generator to prevent a repeat of the incident.

Being Knowledgeable About Claims

At the same time, if you want to be satisfied with the outcome of any claims you file and to obtain the correct amount of compensation, you must become knowledgeable about the process of filing insurance claims and your rights as a policyholder. Possessing such knowledge will enable you to avoid ending up angry and dissatisfied after filing a claim.

You will probably spend in excess of $20,000 on homeowners insurance in your lifetime. And for good reason: to protect property worth many times that amount. Your home and personal property, and the money you spend to insure them, represent the investment of a lot of your dollars. Spending a few hours of your time gaining an understanding of homeowners insurance will serve to keep that money well invested.

If there is one rule that should be kept in mind in dealing with the subject of homeowners insurance, and especially claims, it is that there are no rules. A politician on a radio talk show once said that politics is only a week long, because it changes so fast. And so it is with insurance. Legislators are forever making laws that affect the insurance industry, and these changes frequently take time to trickle down to the attention of the general public. Policies are revised, updated, and changed without the knowledge of consumers. New forms may be adopted and implemented, some of which will supersede older policies. Or an agent or broker may place his business with a new carrier, and switch his customers' policies. Then when notification of such a change is made, the policyholder may put the new policy in a drawer somewhere assuming that it is the same as the old one when it is in fact different.

Claims issues are even more volatile. A court precedent may

only be valid until the next trial date. For example, in one case in California a district court ruled that damage caused by a major flood was not covered, and based its decision on traditional thinking. The appellate court reversed the decision and created a new precedent in the process. One or two cases may completely alter the position of the entire insurance industry on a particular, and perhaps highly important, question. Precedents may also be hazy on some issues as a result of conflicting court decisions. If the rapidly changing rules dictated by court decisions are not enough to make the "right answer" a rarity or a fantasy altogether, the tremendous variation that exists among companies with regard to the handling of claims will certainly do it.

Given the truth that there is no "right answer," no hard, fast rules that can be followed, no road map to a fair and equitable settlement, there is good news and bad news. The good news is that it is not necessary for the layperson to have all of the answers all of the time. Even professionals who spend their lives in the field of insurance sometimes must make judgment calls, without knowing if their position would hold up in court. The bad news, quite simply, is that there is no way that the layperson can know enough about insurance to have the answer to every question that comes up. There is no way to know precisely what route to take to the most satisfactory claim settlement.

Common Sense

Above everything else, the one necessary thing is a vast reservoir of common sense and a kind of open-minded, analytical, inquisitive approach to the issues that come up in dealing with insurance questions. There are experienced people out there in the fields of law and insurance whom one assumes would be well equipped to handle their own claims effectively. Many of them are disappointing in the actual handling of a case and perform lamely, to say the least. There are others who know nothing about law or insurance but who can spot questions and problems way off and resolve their claim to their benefit. The difference is not one of training, education, knowledge, or I.Q. It is a general way of looking at the situation at hand. It is hoped the following chapters will provide you with exposure to the kind of thinking that will enable you to insure your property effectively, and if need be, to pursue a claim.

Insurance, like all specialized and technical fields, has its own jargon. Some knowledge of the language and jargon of the industry and its usage is helpful in dealing with others knowledgeable in the field. This book includes only key terms that are necessary to the understanding of certain aspects of insurance.

Many people view insurance companies as corporate monsters without hearts or feelings, gleefully cashing premium payment checks and awaiting every opportunity to deny claims and minimize settlement amounts. Most insurance companies, however, have a fair approach to the matter of claims, and earnestly desire to provide their customers the protection and compensation they deserve.

In many respects, it is advantageous to society that insurance protection be available. The value of insurance to society is an aspect of the industry that is frequently overlooked. On a small scale, consider the value of insurance protection to the individual homeowner. If homeowners insurance were not available, lending institutions would be unwilling to make loans on property exposed to destruction at the drop of a match. And even if a potential home buyer possessed sufficient funds to purchase a home outright, he would probably have second thoughts about investing such capital in property that could not be protected. On a larger scale, the availability of insurance stimulates investment and growth in business, as risks of loss which would not be acceptable to individual investors are assumed by insurance companies capable of sustaining severe losses.

In Sum

Conclusion

When looking at the subject of insurance in general, keep in mind:

- The value of your insurance protection increases in proportion to your ability to use it effectively.
- To get the most benefit from your insurance, become familiar with the coverage provided by the policy.
- To obtain satisfactory claim settlements, become knowledgeable about the process of filing claims, and your rights as a policyholder.
- The most important factors in approaching insurance questions are common sense and an open mind.
- The field of insurance has its own jargon, and it is helpful to become familiar with it.
- Remember that it is advantageous to society that insurance protection be available, and that insurance companies are not necessarily corporate monsters.

2 How to Shop for Insurance

• Are You a Good Risk? • Getting a Good Deal
• Service Counts • Agents and Brokers

THE best way to get the best "buy" on insurance is to shop for it. When you set out to comparison-shop for insurance, it is important that you consider all your potential risks, and buy insurance that will provide adequate protection for your needs. Just as you would not walk into an automobile dealer's showroom and accept whatever car the salesman suggested, rather you would have in mind the kind of car you want, a color selection, a specific engine size, and possibly a list of options you would like to include. You will be wise to approach the purchase of insurance in a similar manner. Review the differences in the products available, and spend your premium dollars wisely.

Many people mistakenly assume that all homeowners insurance policies are basically the same, and that the policies provide coverage for every conceivable loss. The lesson learned from such a misconception is invariably disappointing and frequently expensive. A friend of mine, for example, mistakenly assumed that his car stereo was covered under his homeowners policy, and therefore did not insure it separately. When the stereo was stolen from his car, he had to pay for a new one out of his own pocket.

As we will see, insurance policies differ tremendously. There are a substantial number of exclusions in every insurance policy, and these, in conjunction with other limiting policy conditions, are responsible for reduced claim payments or denied claims. For this reason, if no other, it is beneficial for you to shop for insurance carefully and conscientiously.

From the outset, it is prudent to consider insuring all property that you cannot afford to risk losing, and to insure such property to its full value. This will enable you to avoid some common pitfalls, such as having inadequate amounts of insurance on certain property, or of not having comprehensive enough coverage on a highly valuable item. Once you purchase a homeowners policy, the cost of tailoring it to fit your specific needs is relatively low. If you want earthquake coverage, for example, the cost of an earthquake endorsement will usually be a fraction of the cost of the initial policy. If you want a floater policy—a policy that insures specific personal property items—the additional cost will probably be minimal.

Are You a Good Risk?

One of the first things that you should know is that certain companies are extremely choosy about the property they insure, preferring to issue policies exclusively on what they refer to as "preferred risks." A preferred risk in a layman's terms is a risk that is desirable to insure because the chances of a loss occurring to the property are minimized by the nature of the property and the applicant. A new home in a neighborhood of increasing property values, which is well maintained and occupied by careful and conscientious individuals, is obviously more desirable to insure than a seventy-five-year-old home with electrical wiring rotting in the walls and old newspapers piled two feet high around the water heater.

The second factor to keep in mind when shopping for insurance is that the claim record of an applicant is a significant factor in assessing the desirability of a risk as well. If, for instance, an applicant has experienced numerous losses with a particular company in a short period of time and appears to be "claims conscious," other companies might hesitate to insure him. If a company carefully screens applicants, and can thereby minimize the number of claims filed by doing so, that company is in a position to provide superior service and to assume a more liberal attitude toward the payment of claims. It is readily understandable that a company that pays ten average size claims for every thousand policies written is under less pressure to minimize payments than a company that pays twenty such claims for each thousand policies issued. Companies following such conservative underwriting practices are also in a position to offer insurance at a lower rate than their competitors simply because they are paying less in claim payments. As a result, it is best to buy insurance from a company that chooses its customers carefully, not only because the price of the product may be less than similar insurance purchased from a company writing more standard business, but also because the service provided by these companies may be superior as well.

The advantage of having a good claim record is that you will be able to obtain insurance from a company underwriting preferred risks. These companies usually have stringent qualification requirements, based on the type of construction of the home involved, its age, location and value, and the claim record of the applicant. And if you meet the requirements, you will be able to buy comprehensive insurance at low rates from a company that will provide good service when necessary. If your claim record makes you an undesirable customer, you will probably have to turn to a company insuring "standard" or "substandard" risks and, as might be expected, such companies are more likely to make collecting on a claim difficult.

Many people think of insurance in the same context as other commodities, and look for ways to get a return on the money spent on premiums. It is readily understandable that it is difficult for a policyholder to have a loss that only slightly exceeds the policy deductible, and to not file a claim for the loss just to avoid having a claim on record. The tough part is knowing that a payment could be collected, and to forego filing the claim anyway. The filing of small claims in the long run may prove to be economically counterproductive. I know of a couple who were insured by a good company at a great price. They filed two small claims in a short period of time and were not able to renew their policy when the time came. Their replacement policy cost them much more than the old one, and I am sure that they are sorry they filed those claims.

A spotted claim record can preclude you from getting insurance from a company that is conservative in its underwriting standards. It can also mean higher premium payments in the future and even nonrenewal of your policy.

Getting a Good Deal

Most people are concerned with the cost of homeowners insurance, and rightfully so. If you desire to save money on insurance, there are several ways of doing so, all of which are effective.

The first and foremost is based on simple common sense. Shop around. Prices for identical policies vary as much as 50 percent from agent to agent and company to company. Ask agents and brokers to explain their coverage. Once you have determined the kinds of coverages you want, call several agencies and brokerages and obtain price quotes from them.

If you have a good claim record, ask about special rates that may be available to preferred customers. Many companies offer such plans, but it may be necessary for you to inquire about them directly to obtain information about them.

Another simple and effective way to save money on insurance is to choose a high deductible. A deductible is a set amount that is automatically subtracted from a loss amount before payment is made, and is essentially part of the loss that is absorbed by the policyholder. By choosing a high deductible, say $500 instead of $100, you can save up to 25 percent on your premium payment. But, by the same token, if you have a loss of $425, you will not be able to collect anything from the insurance company, and will have to absorb the entire loss yourself.

It is also possible to save money on insurance by tailoring coverage to your specific needs. In some cases, the basic coverages provided by standard policies are disadvantageous to the policyholder. For instance, the amount of coverage provided for personal property items is usually 50 percent of the amount of coverage that applies to the dwelling. If you determine that the value of your personal property does not exceed 30 percent of the amount of insurance you carry on the structure, you are paying premiums on insurance you will never be able to collect on. In such a situation, you might search out a company willing to sell you a reduced amount of insurance on your personal property.

Still another way to save money on insurance is to self-insure your property. Property is self-insured when you assume the risk of a loss, instead of passing that risk on to an insurance company. There are times when you might benefit from merely protecting your property in some way that is particularly effective. For instance, you could keep a large amount of expensive jewelry in a safe deposit box, and save the expense of insuring it. The old cliché, "An ounce of prevention is worth a pound of cure," applies to the protection of your property. A snarling

German shepherd and a seven-foot fence are worth a million dollars of theft insurance.

Insurance companies make money by betting that you will not sustain a loss. In most cases, the odds are in their favor, not yours. By self-insuring property you are turning the odds in your favor. You are, on a small scale, reaping profits that would otherwise go to an insurance company.

It should be pointed out that self-insurance is an advantageous plan of action when dealing with items that are of limited value, or those that are easy to protect, such as a service of silver flatware that can be kept in a large safe deposit box. Where extremely valuable items are concerned, such as a rare Early American Windsor chair, it is wise to allow an insurance company to assume the risk of sustaining a large loss.

Service Counts

When shopping for insurance, you will want to consider the reputation of a prospective insurer for providing service when necessary. Obviously, it is advantageous to purchase insurance from a company that approaches claims issues with a liberal attitude. This factor will frequently make the difference between receiving a fair and equitable payment in settlement of a claim and enduring a frustrating and hostile debate with a company representative. A company's approach to the payment of claims can, and often does, result in a difference of hundreds of dollars in the amount of a settlement, even where small claims are concerned.

The best method of obtaining information about a company's reputation for paying claims is to ask around. Your friends and neighbors will frequently have opinions about various insurance companies. Also, this is an area where the opinions of agents and brokers are valuable. They are constantly exposed to company differences, and usually have strong feelings about the service provided by specific companies. The Better Business Bureau in your area will be able to tell you which companies people complain about most frequently; those are the companies to avoid. The State Insurance Commissioner in your state is also a good source of information about the reputations of insurance companies.

Agents and Brokers

While on the subject of shopping for insurance, it is appropriate to examine the role of the individuals involved in selling insurance—the agents and brokers.

Agents and brokers are both involved in selling insurance. The difference between the two is that agents directly represent one or more companies, and have the authority to bind companies to contracts of insurance. Brokers represent the insurance purchaser, and will obtain insurance for a client from one of many insurance companies. Brokers do not have the authority to bind a company to a contract. Some insurance salespeople are both agents and brokers, and might act as agents for some companies and as brokers for still others. Both agents and brokers collect a commission on the business they write, based on a percentage of the amount of premium generated. The usual commission for an agent selling homeowners insurance is 15 to 20 percent. These days, homeowners insurance is usually sold by agents, as brokers tend to be involved predominantly in the sale of commercial policies.

One big difference between agents and brokers is that a broker is more removed and insulated from the activities of an insurance company than an agent. This may limit the company's liability to some extent, if it should take issue with a decision or implication made by a broker. Agents, by contrast, are seen to act with complete authority by some courts, as if there were no distinction between the company and the agent. This means that the company may be bound by the actions of an agent, even though the actions taken were contrary to the desires of the company.

There are essentially two kinds of agents: independent agents, who sell insurance for several different companies while remaining separate entities, and agents who write for one company only and who are directly controlled by that company. Farmers and State Farm are examples of two insurance companies that sell their policies through their own agents. The products and services offered by both kinds of agents are almost identical; you should shop carefully for the best deal.

Some insurance can be purchased directly from the insurance company, without the intervention of an agent or broker. It is merely sold through the mail. The obvious problem with this kind of operation is that you may not have a local representative to go to with a problem or question. The company may be halfway across the country and reachable only by phone. At times, homeowners insurance is purchased on behalf of a property owner by the mortgage company, in order to secure property used as collateral on a loan. The problem here is that you will have no control over the kind of insurance that the mortgage company buys for you.

An agent or broker willing to get involved in your claim and take your side on hazy issues can be very helpful to you. An agent may have a great deal of influence with the underwriters, and consequently with the claims staff, of your company, especially if the agent is responsible for producing a lot of business for that company. Insurance companies typically employ sales people whose job it is to call on insurance agents and get the agent to place business with them. The sales pitch may well involve good service when claims are filed, and a salesperson may have a stake in working within the company to keep your agent happy and to stay in good stead in his territory.

If your agent writes several hundred thousand dollars' worth of business with one particular company, and you are having difficulty with that company on a claim issue, the agent's intervention can be a powerful force. If your agent were to decide to move that business to a different company, your insurance company would lose a substantial chunk of income. As a result of pressure from your agent or broker, a company may be moved to take a more liberal approach to a questionable claim.

In most cases, it will be wholly to your agent's advantage to have you treated well by the company and to have your claims paid promptly and fairly. Your agent wants an army of satisfied customers throughout the community. In most cases, it will be to the agent's advantage to argue your position to the company. The only factor that might make this untrue in a particular case are agents' bonuses. Many companies pay a bonus commission to agents who consistently experience low loss ratios, meaning that little or no money is paid out on claims to those agents' customers. Payment of a large claim, or even a small one if your agent is nearing the bonus cutoff point, may eliminate qualification for a year-end bonus. If your agent seems hesitant to go to bat for you on a claim or even to file a claim that might not be covered, this may be the reason.

You should be willing to take advantage of any help your agent might be able to offer by intervening with the company on your behalf, using influence and bringing pressure to bear. The agent is paid for providing assistance to you and should be willing to work for you when necessary. If your agent knows the business of insurance well, the advice offered will be accurate and valuable. Keep in mind that the company's claims office may have different ideas than your agent on a particular question, and may directly contradict statements made by your agent. Agents are salespeople, not claims people, and their knowledge of claims is often limited. Do not hesitate to seek advice from your agent, but do not depend on your agent to handle your claim or to provide final answers to your questions.

Do your homework and see to it that your questions are resolved properly.

In Sum

As you shop around for the best insurance for you, remember:

- Study the differences in policies carefully, and buy insurance suited to your specific needs.
- Being a good risk for an insurance company can mean better service and cost savings for you.
- A good claim record is always a plus.
- The four ways to save money on homeowners insurance:
    1) comparison shop
    2) choose a high deductible
    3) tailor coverage to your specific needs
    4) consider self-insuring some of your property
- Consider the service reputation of the company with which you place your business.
- Your selection of an agent or broker is important, and can make a difference in the service you receive.

③ The Six Standard Policies

• Various Forms • All Risk and Named Peril • Replacement Cost and Actual Cash Value • The Six Basic Homeowners Policies and How They Differ • Best Policies for Condominium and Cooperative Apartment Owners • 1982 Policy Edition • 1984 Policy Edition

HOMEOWNERS policies, as we know them today, came into being in the 1950s. Prior to that time, homeowners had to buy insurance piece by piece. The typical homeowner had to buy a fire policy to cover possible damage by fire, a liability policy to provide protection for someone being injured on his property, for example, and endorsements to cover additional causes of damage, such as vandalism and theft. The homeowners policies compiled many necessary coverages into one convenient package. These new policies caught on rapidly, as you might suspect, and they quickly became a standard within the insurance industry. These convenient, all-in-one package policies are what we are still using today, although they have

been revised and updated a number of times since their intro-
duction.

Various Forms

There are many kinds of homeowners forms used by insurance
companies, although most are very similar. Differences exist
not only from company to company, but from state to state
as well. These differences are based on legal requirements that
apply in some states. For instance, in some states, such as
California and Colorado, insurance companies are free to use
any kind of homeowners policy they want, as long as the Department of Insurance in that state feels that the policy is not
unfair to the public, and as long as the rates charged for the
product are fair. In most states, however, all homeowners policies must be approved by the Department of Insurance. Some
insurance companies write their own forms, and some modify
already existing policies to suit their needs. The established
industry standard for homeowners policies, however, are those
issued by the Insurance Services Office, also known as the
ISO.

The ISO is a national nonprofit organization serving the
property and casualty insurance industry. The firm is headquar-
tered in New York City, with offices in many large cities around
the country. The ISO develops policies and makes them available to companies that want to use them, for a fee. The essentials
of the homeowners policies produced by the ISO have re-
mained the same for years, although there have been many
changes. The 1971 edition of the homeowners forms were
the standard fare until the ISO introduced the "plain English"
policies in 1976. These forms, called HO–76 policies, are now
used in 80 percent of the states and were purposely created
so that they would be easier for the average person to read

and understand. The writers tried to eliminate much of the technical insurance language of the previous policies and to put the wording into plain English. The 1976 policies are printed in larger type size than the earlier, 1971 forms, and contain some differences in coverages. The 1971 and 1976 editions of the ISO homeowners series contain the essential elements of most of the homeowners policies in use today, and are the foundation for most of them. The vast majority of modern homeowners policies resemble one of the two versions very closely.

At the time of this writing, there are new homeowners policies on the horizon. A 1982 homeowners series was offered on a test basis in several states including Georgia, Colorado, Massachusetts, Oregon, Wisconsin, and California. The 1982 form was a prototype for the 1984 edition of the homeowners policies, introduced in California and Oregon at the end of 1984, and available in most states by the end of 1985. Also, a 1983 edition of the homeowners policies was made available as a stopgap measure to counteract several recent legal developments having to do with the interpretation of all risk policies. The important changes in this policy have been integrated into the 1984 edition. The 1982 and 1984 policies are discussed in detail at the end of this chapter.

Approximately 35 percent of all insurance companies use the standard ISO forms or a slightly modified version of them. Some of the larger companies, like Allstate, State Farm, Farmers, and AAA use their own forms, but they are usually similar to the standard ISO policies. Some of the companies writing their own policies have adopted a "plain English" format, while others adhere to the older format of the 1971 edition, which contains insurance-ese that is difficult to understand. In some states, companies are required to include specific provisions in the policies under state law, and those policies naturally have been modified to contain the necessary wording. It is advantageous for companies to use a standard policy, as it enables decisions on claims to be made based on existing court precedents and established industry practices. Writing new and radically different policies opens the door for new questions, interpretations, and litigation.

If we were embarking upon a discussion of the workings of an automobile, we might choose to examine a certain car that best represents the average car and contains the basic elements of a modern automobile. We would all the while realize that not all cars are exactly like the one we were studying, and might look at some of the more significant differences. Let us look at homeowners insurance policies in the same manner.

Since the ISO homeowners policies are the undisputed standard in the industry, they are the obvious choice for our subject of study. The fact that a tremendous amount of case law and discussion has been generated by these forms also contributes to their value as examples for our examination.

All Risk and Named Peril

Before we look at the six standard policies that make up the ISO homeowners series, it is essential that we take the time to understand two key insurance terms that concern coverage and valuation.

The first terms, "all risk" and "named peril," are used to connotate types of insurance coverage. All risk coverage means that it protects against loss by *any* cause, except those specifically excluded. Named peril coverage means it insures against specific perils listed in the policy.

The coverage provided by named peril homeowners policies varies, as you will see, among the forms available, and the covered perils refer to both the real and personal property covered in most cases.

Replacement Cost and Actual Cash Value

The second key insurance term to understand is "valuation." It refers to the method used to establish the amount that the policy will pay for insured property that is damaged by a covered peril. Payment will be based on the "replacement cost" of the property, or on the "actual cash value" of the property, whichever the policy calls for. Replacement cost simply means that the company is responsible for the full cost of repair or replacement of the damaged property, without deducting for improvement or depreciation. Actual cash value is a term which is somewhat difficult to define. With respect to personal property, actual cash value is based on replacement cost less depreciation. With respect to buildings, actual cash value can be based on numerous factors, including physical condition, age, obsolescence, market value, and other factors influencing the value of the building. In homeowners policies, valuation is at actual cash value unless the policy specifies that replacement cost coverage is provided. The concepts of actual cash value and depreciation are expanded upon in later chapters.

The Six Basic Homeowners Policies and How They Differ

What follows is a synopsis of the coverage offered by each of the six basic policies.

HO–1 and HO–2 Forms

Both the HO–1 and HO–2 are named peril policies with the same perils applicable to the dwelling and personal property coverages.

The HO–1 insures against the following perils:

- fire or lightning
- removal (of damaged property and property under threat of damage by a named peril). This might include the cost of

removing personal property from a house when a neighboring
house is burning and there is a danger that the fire will spread.
- windstorm or hail
- explosion
- riot or civil commotion
- vehicles or aircraft damage to dwellings and personal property
- smoke damage
- vandalism or malicious mischief
- breakage of glass
- theft

In the policy form, each of these named perils is followed
by a paragraph of explanations, most containing numerous
exclusions that apply.

The HO–1 is being used less and less, and it will soon be
unavailable altogether in some states. The most attractive feature of the HO–1 is its low cost, but this feature is offset by
the limited coverage provided by the form. A good example
of the problems that can result from such limited coverage is
the story of an elderly couple on a fixed income who bought
the policy in order to save money. One of them accidentally
allowed a bathtub to overflow for a long period of time, resulting in severe damage to the plaster ceiling and walls of the
room below the bathtub, as well as to the carpet and some
personal property items. The loss was not covered under the
HO–1, whereas it would have been covered under any of the
other homeowners policies in the series.

The HO–2 form insures against:

- fire or lightning
- removal (as defined above)
- windstorm or hail
- explosion
- riot or civil commotion
- aircraft damage to dwellings and personal property
- vehicle damage to dwellings and personal property

- sudden and accidental damage from smoke
- vandalism or malicious mischief
- breakage of glass
- theft
- falling objects
- weight of ice, snow, or sleet
- collapse of buildings
- sudden and accidental rupture of steam or hot water heating systems, such as a water heater rupturing
- accidental discharge or overflow of water or steam from within a plumbing appliance
- freezing of plumbing, heating, air-conditioning, and domestic appliances
- sudden and accidental injury from electrical currents artificially generated

The perils listed in the forms mentioned above are followed by conditions and exclusions, but in the HO-2 form the exclusions are not as extensive as those in the HO-1. The HO-2 form is designated the "broad form," in that it affords greater coverages than the HO-1. In addition to the more comprehensive coverage of the HO-2, and the differences in the exclusions that apply, some of the other notable differences between the two policies are:

- The HO-1 limits glass coverage to $50 per occurrence, while the HO-2 does not.
- The 1971 edition of the HO-1 limits coverage relative to smoke damage to "direct loss from smoke due to a sudden, unusual, and faulty operation of any heating or cooking unit in or on the described premises but excluding smoke from fireplaces." Note that the damage must result from a sudden, unusual, and faulty operation of an appliance. *All* criteria must be met. The HO-2 covers all smoke damage, "other than smoke from agricultural smudging or industrial operations." The only stipulation is that the loss be "sudden and accidental." In the 1976 edition of the HO-1, the coverage for smoke damage is the same as the HO-2.

- The HO–1 excludes loss by vehicles owned or driven by any occupant of the premises. The HO–2 excludes only loss to fences, driveways, and walks by a vehicle owned or operated by an occupant of the premises.

Although the HO–2 provides more comprehensive coverage than the HO–1, there are still many limitations to the coverage. An illustration of this limited coverage is the case of the homeowner who decided to paint his own house. While painting a second-story section of the house, he accidentally kicked over a five-gallon bucket of paint that was sitting on the roof next to him. The paint ran down the roof, into the rain gutters, and down the front of the house as well. His loss was not covered under his HO–2 policy, while it would have been covered under an all risk policy.

HO–3 Forms

The HO–3 is the most common homeowners policy in the series. It provides all risk, replacement cost coverage to the dwelling. Personal property is also insured against named perils, as listed in the policy. These perils are basically the same as the ones listed relative to the HO–2 policy, although they have been modified slightly to suit the HO–3 form.

The HO–3 policy offers all risk coverage on the dwelling. This is a particularly valuable feature and is a key to what sets the HO–3 apart from the HO–1 and HO–2. The scope of claims that may be paid under the policy is considerable. For example, accidental spillage of paint on carpeting would be covered, as would accidental burns on a kitchen countertop where no fire is involved, the burns being caused by a hot frying pan or an electric iron. This all risk policy would also cover the leaking of rainwater into the interior of a dwelling through a worn roof even though there had been no damage to the roof by wind. Even damage caused by stray golf balls hit by politicians or other well-meaning individuals would be covered! And if you were to gouge a hole in a wall while hauling out an old washing machine, you would have coverage under the HO–3 policy.

An amusing example of the value of the all risk coverage provided by the HO–3 is the homeowner who ran into trouble while moving a piano. He set up a wooden ramp over two steps in a small hallway and planned, with the help of his two children, to roll the piano on a dolly from the living room to the den. When he moved the piano onto the ramp, he found that the weight was more than he could control and the piano rolled down the ramp, across the kitchen floor, and into the kitchen cabinets. The damage to the piano itself was not covered, but the damage to the house was, under the all risk coverage.

As with the HO–1 and HO–2, the HO–3 policy is subject to extensive exclusions. In the 1971 edition, the exclusions apply to both buildings and personal property, but in the 1976 policies, the exclusions refer separately to buildings and personal property. However, the effect is the same. The HO–3 exclusions include loss caused by or resulting from:

- flood
- surface water (natural water after it touches the ground)
- waves, tidal waves, overflow of streams or other bodies of water
- water which backs up through sewers or drains. This is commonly held to mean stoppages in city sewer or drainage systems, and not stoppages within the plumbing or rain gutters located on the insured premises. If flood or surface water flows in and out of a clogged drain, it loses its definition as flood or surface water, and it could be argued that the damage caused by it would be covered, not excluded, if the stoppage is on the premises.
- water below the surface of the ground, including that which exerts pressure on or flows, seeps, or leaks through sidewalks,

driveways, foundations, walls, basements, or other floors or through doors, windows, or any other openings in sidewalks, driveways, foundations, walls, or floors. This refers to surface water—accidental admission of water that is not surface water is covered.

- earth movement, earthquake, volcanic eruption, landslide, mud flow, earth sinking, rising or shifting. The 1976 policy merely excludes "earth movement," which is intended to encompass all of these phenomena.
- damage to plumbing, heating, or air-conditioning systems, or damage caused by leakage from them, when the damage results from freezing of the systems and the building has been vacant, unless safeguards have been taken to protect against this kind of damage.
- wear and tear
- marring or scratching
- deterioration
- inherent vice, latent defect, mechanical breakdown
- rust
- mold
- wet or dry rot
- contamination
- smog
- acts of war
- nuclear reactions
- acts of governments
- smoke from agricultural smudging or industrial operations
- settling, cracking, shrinkage, bolting, or expansion of pavements, patios, foundations, walls, floors, roofs, or ceilings
- birds, vermin, rodents, insects, domestic animals
- continuous seepage or leakage from within a plumbing system or domestic appliance. The 1971 policy specifies that coverage does not apply if the condition persists for more than two weeks. The newer edition merely specifies "a period of time."
- theft in or to a dwelling under construction, including building materials and supplies, until the building is completed and occupied
- vandalism and glass breakage if the property has been vacant

for longer than thirty consecutive days immediately preceding the loss. A dwelling is considered vacant if it is devoid of furniture and inhabitants. If there are furnishings in the dwelling but no inhabitants, the structure is merely unoccupied. The dwelling has to be vacant for thirty consecutive days. If the dwelling has been visited by any person during that thirty-day period for any reason, it can be argued that the dwelling was not vacant.

- wind, hail, ice, snow, or sleet damage to: outdoor radio and television antennas, including wiring, masts, and towers
- Certain losses resulting from excluded perils are covered. The older forms state that losses by fire, smoke, explosion, building collapse, glass breakage, or water "not otherwise excluded" are covered, if they result from the excluded perils listed. The new forms merely state that an ensuing loss that is not excluded is covered. For example, if the bearings in an appliance motor were to deteriorate, burn out the motor, and start a fire, coverage for the ensuing fire would be provided, although coverage for the bearings would not because they would be considered damaged by deterioration.

HO–5 Forms

The HO–5 policy is similar to the HO–3 in that the dwelling is covered on an all risk basis. Personal property, however, is covered under all risk conditions also. This is the primary difference between the HO–3 and the HO–5. In the 1971 edition of the homeowners policies, the HO–5 provides a greater amount of coverage for personal property away from the insured premises than the HO–3, but in the 1976 edition, the amount of insurance available for property away from the premises is the same in both policies.

The HO–5 policy is clearly the most comprehensive standard homeowners form available. However, premiums charged for this coverage are high, and the added protection may not be worth the cost. The HO–5 is another policy that is rarely used these days. Some agents attach an endorsement to an HO–3 policy that provides all risk coverage to personal property, instead of using an HO–5.

To illustrate the value of all risk coverage to personal property provided by the HO–5, let us consider the case of a policyholder who was a father and a computer owner. One of his small children spilled a glass of milk into the keyboard of his expensive computer, ruining the keyboard. This loss was covered under his HO–5 policy, whereas it would not be covered under any of the other homeowners policies in the series.

The HO–3 is typically felt to be the best value of all of the homeowners policies for the average person. The protection provided is comprehensive, and the replacement cost coverage is a big plus. Recently, many companies have begun to offer replacement cost coverage to personal property by endorsement. Such an endorsement, which will usually provide highly valuable coverage for a very reasonable price, attached to an HO–3 policy makes for an effective package of insurance.

Best Policies for Condominium and Cooperative Apartment Owners

HO–4 and HO–6 Policies

The HO–4 is a tenant homeowners policy, designed for people who rent houses or apartments, and also usually applies to owners of cooperative apartments. The HO–6 is a condominium owners policy. The policies are very similar. Both forms cover personal property and improvements to the residence made by the policyholder. Improvements are defined as any cosmetic addition made to a unit, such as paneling, shelves, and the like. The HO–4 affords coverage up to 10 percent of the amount of the policy for improvements. This means that if your personal property is insured for $10,000 under an HO–4, $1,000 would apply to cover improvements to the dwelling that you had installed. The HO–6 form affords a straight $1,000 worth of coverage for improvements, additions, and alterations regardless of the amount of the policy limits.

Neither the HO–4 nor the HO–6 provides coverage for building structures, or for building items not installed by the policyholder. In the case of condominiums, each owner insures his own structure, or the structure and public areas are insured by an owners association. Cooperative apartment structures are insured by the corporation that owns the cooperative. In any case, the owner's personal property and improvements to his own structure are insured under an HO–6 or an HO–4.

Problems sometimes arise when condominium or co-op unit owners fail to insure the parts of the building for which they are responsible. Often the owner is expected to assume responsibility for the interior walls, floors, cabinets, and the like. This kind of coverage is available, but is not included in the standard HO–4 or HO–6 policy. Some agents merely write HO–3 policies on condominiums and co-op units to eliminate potential gaps in coverage.

An example of a problem resulting from this kind of gap in coverage is the condominium unit owner who had a severe fire in his unit. He had an HO–6 policy and assumed that he was fully covered. After the fire, the owners association's insurance company said they would pay for the structural part of the building, but not for the interior finish items like flooring, paneling, or cabinets. The unit owner's company said that the HO–6 covered only his personal property, and allowed $1,000 for improvements he had installed in the unit. Since he had not installed any of the interior finish items in the unit, the policyholder was unable to collect from either company for these items. Needless to say, he absorbed a tremendous uninsured loss.

Another incident involving a severe fire illustrates the effect of the limitation on improvements. A tenant in an apartment building spent thousands of dollars redecorating the unit and, after the fire, found that only a fraction of the cost of the redecorating would be recoverable under his insurance policy.

Both forms are named peril forms, meaning property is insured for damage resulting from certain perils. Under the HO–4 and HO–6 forms, personal property is insured against:

- fire or lightning
- removal
- windstorm or hail
- explosion
- riot or civil commotion
- aircraft
- vehicles
- smoke
- vandalism or malicious mischief
- theft
- falling objects
- weight of ice, snow, or sleet
- collapse of buildings
- damage from hot water heating systems
- damage from plumbing and appliances
- damage from freezing of plumbing appliances
- damage from electrical currents artificially generated

Protection for these perils is subject to many of the conditions, limitations, and exclusions applicable under the other HO policies.

Payment under both the HO–4 and HO–6 forms is based on the actual cash value of the property damaged, not on the replacement cost.

1982 Policy Edition

As mentioned earlier, the 1982 ISO homeowners policies are available in a few states on a test basis. The companies using the policies have been surveyed, and the policies have been revised and have evolved into the 1984 homeowners series.

In all probability, these new policies will become the industry standard in the near future.

The 1982 policies are essentially a revision of the 1976 forms and are very similar. Some significant differences between the 1982 edition and the 1976 edition are:

The special limits of liability on certain property have been raised to keep pace with inflation. The limitation on personal property such as money, bank notes, and precious metals has been raised to $200. The coverage on all property subject to a $500 limit has been increased to $2,500, with the limit on firearms raised to $2,000.

A total of $500 is provided to remove fallen trees from the premises if the trees are damaged by perils that do not apply to trees, or if the trees are not covered by the policy. (An example would be the case of a neighbor's tree that falls on your property.)

The exclusion of loss by theft of property from an unattended vehicle or boat has been omitted. This means that there do not have to be signs of forced entry into a locked boat or vehicle in order for a theft to be covered.

Personal liability coverage has been raised to a standard amount of $100,000, and the limits on medical payments to others have been raised from $500 to $1,000.

The limits on water craft and their trailers and equipment have been raised from $500 to $1,000.

Coverage for damage to property of others has been increased from $250 to $500, with replacement cost coverage applicable.

An additional amount of insurance is available in some cases for debris removal.

There is a new definition of earth movement in the exclusions section of the policy, which includes volcanic eruption.

The standard deductible has been raised from $100 to $250.

Coverage is provided for losses resulting from the theft or unauthorized use of bank electronic fund transfer cards.

Coverage for losses resulting when you lend a motor vehicle

to someone else is specifically excluded. As a result of court rulings, this coverage sometimes applied under the wording in the 1976 policies, although the policy underwriters never intended to provide such coverage.

Coverage is provided in the amount of $1,000 for assessments to homeowners as a result of losses to property owned as part of a corporation or association with others.

1984 Policy Edition

The 1984 policies include most of the changes in the 1982 edition as well as other changes. The significant changes are:

Coverage for business property has been included, with limits of $2,500 for property on the premises, and $250 for property off the premises.

In addition to the full limits on personal liability, coverage is also provided for prejudgment interest on damage awards.

Cooperative apartment owners can be insured under the 1984 HO–6 form as well as the HO–4. The previous HO–6 policies were intended to be written only on condominiums.

A specific exclusion applies that precludes coverage for any loss caused intentionally by any insured. The prior forms do not exclude coverage for insureds not participating in the intentional act.

The policy excludes faulty, inadequate, or defective planning, construction, or maintenance, as well as acts or decisions of people or government bodies.

The policy includes limiting the degree of coverage for the peril of building collapse. In effect, loss resulting from collapse is covered only when caused by specified perils.

The term all risk will no longer be used in the insuring agreement. The word "all" will be eliminated, and the policy will merely specify coverage for risk of direct physical loss. It is misleading to include the word "all," which has contributed to the liberal interpretation of the policies by courts. It is intended that the coverage be the same as that originally contemplated in the all risk policies, before that coverage was broadened by court rulings.

Most existing homeowners policies contain a liberalization clause, which stipulates that if the insurance company broadens its current homeowners policy each policyholder is entitled to any broadening of coverage provided by the new endorsement. If your company adopts a new version of the homeowners policy, you will not, however, benefit from the expansion of coverage until you renew your existing policy.

In Sum

As you consider the subjects of coverage and valuation, keep in mind:

- Although most insurance policies are similar, there are significant differences, and each policy must be studied on its own.
- The terms "all risk" and "named peril" describe the types of coverage that apply to most property insured under homeowners policies.
- The term "valuation" refers to the method used to establish the amount that the policy will pay for insured property that is damaged by a covered peril.
- There are six basic homeowners policies that comprise the standard homeowners series.
- There is a new 1984 edition of the homeowners policies available in some areas. These new policies will most likely become a new industry standard within a couple of years.

4 Walking Through a Policy in Terms of Coverages

• Property and Interests Covered • Basic Amounts of Coverage • Supplementary or Additional Coverages • Deductibles • Personal Liability • Medical Payments to Others • Umbrella Policies • Damage to Property of Others

THE best way to gain an understanding of the coverage provided by a homeowners policy is to take a walk through one, stopping to look at and examine the coverage offered.

Property and Interests Covered

The first step in examining the coverage included in a homeowners policy is to look at the four types of property and interests covered. They are:

1. The Dwelling—Known as Coverage A

The dwelling coverage includes the dwelling described in the policy plus any additions and structures connected to it, such as a garage, carport, etc. (By way of illustration, a breezeway would be considered part of the dwelling if it is connected to it.) It is also stipulated that the dwelling must be occupied principally as a private, occupied residence. Homeowners policies are intended to cover *owner-occupied* residences only and not commercial buildings. A house used exclusively as an office, studio, or other business facility cannot rightfully be insured under a homeowners policy, and such a situation can create problems if a claim is filed, and may even preclude coverage.

Along with the dwelling, materials and supplies on the premises or "adjacent thereto" are also covered. This is a rather ambiguous phrase, and can refer to property on a neighboring lot or on a street next to the insured dwelling. The policy states that there must be an intention to use the materials and supplies within a reasonable time at the described location. Building materials merely stored at the premises do not qualify for coverage.

In the 1971 edition of the homeowners policy, the dwelling coverage also includes building equipment, fixtures, and outdoor equipment pertaining to the service of the premises while at the described premises or located elsewhere temporarily, providing this property is owned by the insured and is not "otherwise covered." Fixtures and equipment are defined as follows:

- "Outdoor equipment" includes lawn mowers, small tractors, outdoor furniture, gas barbecues, etc.
- "Building equipment" can include propane and oil tanks, storm windows, tools used to maintain the property, and similar items.
- "Fixtures" are personal property that are considered real property when permanently attached to the building, and may

include such items as blinds, shades, mirrors, built-in shelves, awnings, and other such property.

Building equipment, fixtures, and outdoor equipment must pertain to the service of the premises. For example, a forklift intended for use in a policyholder's business would not qualify as outdoor equipment pertaining to the service of the premises. The term "premises" here is intended to include the entire lot the dwelling is situated on, and equipment and fixtures used to service all of the property. It would include such items as horse stables, swimming pools, patios, driveways, brick walks, etc.

The policy covers fixtures and equipment as defined while away from the premises "temporarily." There is no commonly held interpretation of this term within the insurance industry, and it is not defined in the policy, yet it is rather self-explanatory.

Rented or borrowed property is not covered under the dwelling coverage, as the property covered must be owned by the insured. We will see, however, that rented or borrowed personal property is covered under another section of the policy.

Also, property included in this section is covered only "when not otherwise covered." In many instances, building equipment and outdoor equipment will be covered as personal property, although it is possible that the limits on same could be exhausted, at which time such property would be covered under the dwelling coverage.

2.   Appurtenant or Other Structures—Known as Coverage B

Coverage B provides insurance for detached structures. There are several conditions that an appurtenant or other structure must meet in order to be considered such by an insurance policy. The 1976 version of the policy states that the structure must be separated from the dwelling by a "clear space," and that structures connected by a fence or utility line are other structures, and not part of the dwelling. This stipulation is not included in the older 1971 form, but is generally accepted anyway. Undoubtedly the new language was included in the 1976 form to eliminate the question of when a structure is part of the dwelling and when it is a separate, detached structure.

In both the 1971 and 1976 homeowners policy editions, an exclusion applies to structures used in whole or in part for business purposes. This means that any business use, no matter how small, precludes coverage. For example, a structure used for a small real estate office would not be covered. The 1971 edition states that the structure must pertain to the use and occupancy of the dwelling as a residence. This stipulation has been omitted in the 1976 edition because if a structure is not used for private use, it must be used for a business purpose.

Structures rented or leased or held for rental or lease are also excluded, unless the structures in question are rented to a tenant of the dwelling or are used as private garages. Under both policies, materials and supplies located on or near the premises for construction or alteration of detached structures are covered.

The amounts of insurance that apply to the property and interests covered in the homeowners policies are based on a percentage of the amount of insurance that applies to the dwelling. Structures are insured for 10 percent of the amount of insurance that applies to the dwelling. If your home is insured for $100,000, the amount of insurance available to cover appurtenant or other structures is $10,000.

3. Personal Property—Known as Coverage C

Personal property covered includes such items as clothes and furniture owned or used by an insured anywhere in the

world, as well as property owned by others while located at
a portion of the premises occupied by an insured. This coverage
also applies to property away from the described premises,
as long as the property is owned by a guest of the insured
or a residence employee, and is in a residence occupied by
an insured. The 1971 form specifies that the property must
be usual to the occupancy of the premises as a dwelling to
be covered, and the newer policy does not include this language,
as business property is addressed elsewhere in the form.

In all of the 1971 policies except the HO–5, there is a limit
on property away from the premises of 10 percent of the
amount of insurance on personal property, but never less than
$1,000. This means that if $50,000 is available to cover personal property, $5,000 would apply to property away from
the premises. This limit is greatly broadened in the 1976 policies, with the full limit on personal property available on property away from the premises. The only limitation applies to
property normally situated at a secondary residence of the
policyholder, such as a mountain cabin or summer home. The
limit that applies is again 10 percent of the amount of insurance
on personal property.

Numerous exclusions apply to personal property alone. Personal property coverage excludes:

- Animals, birds, and fish of the insured or anyone else.
- Motorized vehicles, except those used for the service of the
  premises and not licensed for road use.
- Property of roomers and boarders not related to the insured.
- Business property held for sale or delivery, or sales samples
- Property rented to others by the policyholder, or held for
  rental to others. This does not apply to property and furnish-
  ings located in a part of the dwelling rented to boarders.
- Business property while away from the described premises.
  This applies to property that is strictly business property that
  is never used by the policyholder for personal or recreational
  use. A painter's airless sprayer would be excluded, for exam-

ple, as it is strictly business property, while a carpenter's tools might be covered if they are used as household property also. Note that business property at the described premises is covered. The 1976 policy edition also specifically excludes business property pertaining to a business conducted at the insured location.

- Auto tape decks and radios. Tapes are not covered when in a vehicle.
- Property insured by other insurance (such as business insurance).

The following exclusions refer to personal property (some to loss by theft specifically), and are outlined in the "Perils Insured Against" section of the policy. They are included here for the sake of organization. The policy excludes:

- Loss caused by rain or snow entering the dwelling, unless the rain or snow enters through an opening made by wind or hail.
- Loss to watercraft (except rowboats and canoes by wind or hail) when not inside fully enclosed buildings.
- Loss by falling objects to property within a building, unless the building is first damaged by the same falling object.
- Loss by rupture of various heating systems caused by or resulting from freezing.
- Loss to tubes, transistors, and other electronic components caused by artificially generated electrical currents.
- Theft of materials from a building under construction.
- The 1971 edition of the policy excludes theft of credit cards, checks, and loss resulting from the misuse of them. The 1976 form provides coverage for such loss, as discussed under "supplementary and additional coverages."
- Theft of a stone from a setting. The 1971 policy edition excludes the theft of a stone from its setting, while the 1976 form does not.
- The 1971 form also excludes theft of personal property when stolen from an unattended vehicle, unless visible marks of forced entry into a locked vehicle are evident. An endorsement

is available that eliminates the criterion of forced entry into a locked vehicle. This coverage is frequently attached automatically by some agents, and is also included in some modern forms. The endorsement is extremely inexpensive, and will protect your golf clubs when you stop at the market for a six-pack.

When the insured premises is rented to others, numerous exclusions apply relative to valuable and frequently stolen items like jewelry, money, valuable metals, etc. Also, many exclusions apply to property away from the described premises. Property is covered in a temporary residence, such as a mountain cabin, only when a policyholder is temporarily residing at the location.

There is a section of the homeowners policy that places limits on certain kinds of personal property. These limitations are important, and should be carefully examined. The kinds of property included are those that are valuable and frequently stolen, and failure to consider this one portion of the homeowners policy can result in a tremendous amount of financial loss, and heartbreak as well. I remember one woman who had been given a full-length mink coat for her twenty-fifth wedding anniversary by her husband. She was devastated when the coat was stolen and could not be replaced.

The limits are:

- A total of $100 on money, bullion, bank notes, and numismatic property (coins).
- A total of $500 on securities, deeds, accounts, evidences of debt, notes other than bank notes, letters of credit, passports, tickets, and stamps (including stamp collections).
- A total of $500 on watercraft, including trailers, equipment, furnishings, and outboard motors.
- A total of $500 on trailers.
- A total of $500 in the aggregate, *for loss by theft* of jewelry, furs, watches, precious and semiprecious stones.
- Gold and platinum are limited to $500 in the 1971 form, and to $100 in the 1976 edition.

- Manuscripts are limited to $1,000 in the 1971 form, and $500 in the 1976 form.

Additional limitations in the 1976 policy also include:

- Silver is limited to $100, with silver and goldware limited to $1,000. This not only includes silver and gold, but also plated silver and goldware, and pewter. No such limitation exists in the 1971 form.
- $500 on grave markers.
- $1,000 for loss by theft of guns.

The foregoing limitations are inclusive. This means that you could lose jewelry, furs, watches, and precious stones as a result of theft, and receive only $500 in payment. This $500 limitation does not apply to each respective item, but to the items as a group. This is why it is important to study carefully the limits placed on certain kinds of personal property.

Coverage for personal property is provided in an amount equal to 50 percent of the dwelling limit. If a dwelling is covered for $100,000, $50,000 would be allowed to cover personal property.

4. Loss of Use or Additional Living Expenses— Known as Coverage D

The "loss of use" coverage is intended to come into play when the insured dwelling is rendered untenantable by a covered loss, such as a fire. The policy covers the necessary "additional" expenses that enable the policyholder to maintain his normal standard of living after a loss. Liability under this coverage is based upon the time required to repair the property "as soon as possible," or to settle the insured's household in permanent quarters, whichever is less.

For this coverage to apply, there must be physical damage to covered property by a covered peril. Consequential or remote losses are not covered.

Further, the policy covers only "necessary" increases in living expenses, not those that may be merely desired by the policyholder.

Under this coverage, the term "additional" is highly relevant. This refers to expenses over and above the policyholder's normal household budget, such as the rent he might have to pay for a temporary apartment or a motel over and above his existing mortgage payment. The cost of having to eat in restaurants would also be included. The coverage is not intended to pay for additional mortgage interest rates, higher house payments, and the like if a policyholder's house is destroyed and he has to buy another one.

Furthermore, the criterion considered is the normal standard of living for the insured's household, and not that of the richer Jones family down the block.

In addition, the extent of this coverage is limited to the actual time required to repair the property, which does not necessarily mean the time taken. This effectively means the amount of time that it would reasonably take to repair the dwelling with diligence and dispatch. Extraneous factors, such as carpenters' strikes and the like that may delay construction, will not necessarily increase the time allowance provided under this provision. The same goes for relocation. Diligence and dispatch are expected, and inordinate delays are to be avoided. In the case of a severe loss, it is usually beneficial for the family to move into permanent quarters as soon as possible.

In addition, real or potential income from rental properties that are damaged is also provided under the loss of use coverage, and is subject to similar restrictions as those just mentioned relative to the time allowed for completing repairs. Saved expenses, such as reductions in utility bills, are to be subtracted from the rental value loss.

When a neighboring building is damaged by a covered peril, and access to the insured premises is prohibited by a civil authority, additional living expense coverage applies for a maximum of two weeks.

Additional living expense coverage is provided in an amount equal to 20 percent of the total policy limit (except in the case of the HO-1 policy, where the amount is 10 percent of the total policy limit). If a policy had a limit of $100,000, then $20,000 would be allowed to cover additional living expenses.

Basic Amounts of Coverage

The standard amounts of coverage provided under the homeowners policies are not perfect for every policyholder. For example, many people do not own personal property that is worth half as much as the cost of replacing their home. This means that many people are required to buy an excessive amount of insurance on personal property. As I previously mentioned, some companies permit the limit on personal property to be lowered to 40 percent of the dwelling limit, with a corresponding reduction in cost. This limit can also be raised by endorsement.

The amount of coverage available for structures is less than ideal in many cases, as well. If a structure is improved in any way, such as for use as a pool house, workshop, recreation room, or the like, the applicable limit of 10 percent of the dwelling amount may be insufficient. A problem of this kind can be solved by purchasing additional insurance on the structure involved.

The amounts of insurance that apply to the property and interests described in the policy in actual fact represent additional amounts of insurance. Let us use a $100,000 policy as an example. The policy would provide:

$100,000 for the dwelling
$ 10,000 for appurtenant or other structures
$ 50,000 for personal property
$ 20,000 for additional living expenses
$180,000 = TOTAL AMOUNT OF INSURANCE AVAILABLE

As you can see, the full limit on each category can be collected over and above the maximum limits on the other coverages.

Supplementary or Additional Coverages

This section of the policy provides coverage for removal of property, debris removal, and fire department service charges. In the 1976 edition it covers reasonable repairs, plants, misuse of credit cards, forgery, and counterfeit money.

The removal coverage provides coverage to property moved from the premises because it is in danger of being damaged by a covered peril, such as a collection of valuable porcelain moved from your house when threatened by a hurricane or tornado. In the 1971 edition, this section also refers to property that is being moved to a new residence, and limitations are placed on the coverage. The amount of insurance available is based on the value of the property at the insured premises versus the value of the property at the new location. And the removed property is covered for a total of 10 percent of the limit on personal property while in transit. The 1976 form provides the full limit on personal property to removed property at the new location as well as while in transit. Both forms limit this coverage to thirty days.

Coverage for debris removal applies to actual expenses incurred, and only refers to covered property damaged by a covered peril. This coverage would not apply to the cost of removing a tree that blew down, for example, as trees are not covered for damage by wind. In the 1976 form, an additional amount of insurance of 5 percent of the limit on the affected property applies to this coverage.

The fire department service charge coverage makes $250 available to pay fire department fees when there is a charge as a result of the insured's liability, "assumed by contract or agreement." In order for this coverage to apply, the fire department must be called to the scene (this rules out voluntary inspections). The 1971 edition requires that there be an actual fire in order for this coverage to apply, and not just smoke or suspicion of fire.

In the 1976 edition, coverage for trees, shrubs, and plants is provided in this section. Coverage is for specified perils only, and a limit of 5 percent of the amount of coverage on the dwelling applies. A limit of $500 for any one plant applies as well. In the 1971 form, the limitations on plants are listed in the "Additional Conditions" section of the policy, and the limit is $250 per plant.

The 1976 edition also includes coverage for misuse of credit cards, forgery, and counterfeit money. The limit on this coverage is $500, and is based on the legal obligation of the policyholder. Certain exclusions and provisions apply to this coverage.

Deductibles

All of the homeowners policies include a loss deductible that will apply to almost every loss that is covered. A deductible is an amount of money that is subtracted from the amount of a loss and must be absorbed by the policyholder. The deductible applies one time to each loss experienced—but not to each item damaged.

The term "loss deductible" means that the deductible is subtracted from the amount of the loss, as opposed to the amount of the claim or the amount otherwise collectible. If you have a loss on property that is subject to a limit, and if the full amount of the loss is not covered for this reason, the entire deductible might not be considered in a real sense. The following example will clarify the way the loss deductible works:

Assume that you have a theft of jewelry items, and that the value of the jewelry is $1,000. Further assume that a limit of $500 applies to loss by theft of jewelry and that you have a $250 deductible. The $250 deductible would be subtracted from the amount of the loss, which is $1,000, leaving $750. You would then be paid the full limit on the property involved, which is $500.

When paying a claim that involves property subject to a limit, the company is only obligated to pay the lowest of the three following amounts:

1. The amount of loss
2. The amount of loss less the deductible
3. The amount of loss on property not subject to a limit, plus the full limit on all property subject to a limit

There are two primary kinds of loss deductibles that apply under homeowners policies: flat deductibles and disappearing deductibles. Some states, notably Texas, have percentage deductibles.

A "flat" deductible is subtracted directly from the amount of the loss, regardless of size. If you were to have a fire in your kitchen, with a cost to repair of $3,000, the amount of your deductible, which might be $250, would be subtracted from the cost to repair, and you would be paid $2,750. Each time you had a loss, even if the losses were, say, only a day apart, the same $250 deductible would apply. There are exceptions to this rule. Storm damage that occurs on different days during the same storm is almost always considered to be the result of one loss, and only one deductible applies.

By contrast, a "disappearing" deductible applies to small losses—those from $50 to $500. When a loss is over $50, the company pays 111 percent of the amount of the loss over

$50 (LOSS − $50 × 111% = AMOUNT PAID). For example, a $250 loss would be paid as follows: $250 − $50 = $200 × 111% = $222. When a disappearing deductible applies, losses under $50 are not covered. When a $100 disappearing deductible applies, the company pays 125 percent of the amount of the loss over $100, and losses under $100 are not covered.

With this kind of deductible, the amount subtracted from the loss decreases as the loss amount approaches $500. The formula would result in payments higher than $500, when the loss amount is over $500. Disappearing deductibles are becoming less common than the flat deductible, primarily because of the rising costs of processing small claims.

Personal Liability

Standard homeowners policies include coverage for comprehensive personal liability. Under Section II of the policy, a standard amount of $25,000 in coverage is provided for general liability. This coverage is intended to protect policyholders from paying for mishaps for which they are liable, and covers the amounts that policyholders become legally liable to pay because of bodily injury or property damage, to which the policy applies.

The coverage applies only when the insured is legally liable. This liability must be demonstrated, not merely implied, and there must be negligence on the part of the policyholder before legal liability can exist. For example, if you were to build some new front stairs, and a guest were to fall through them and be injured, you would be liable for the injury. The final decision on a legal liability question will always rest with the courts. Also, there must be actual property damage or bodily injury resulting from the occurrence. Under this coverage:

• Damages that result in a loss of business, or interruption of business activities, are not covered.

- The insurance company is obligated to defend the policy-holder against suits involving claims that would be covered if the allegations made were true, regardless of whether the allegations are actually true or not and whether liability exists.
- The insurance company has the right to settle a claim without the consent of the policyholder.

Medical Payments to Others

The standard homeowners policy includes coverage for medical payments. This includes coverage for injury to any person while on the insured premises caused by "an accident," and away from the premises if the injury is caused by an insured, or an insured's resident employee in the course of employment, or is caused by an animal owned by or in the care of an insured. Coverage also applies if injury is sustained by a third party arising out of the condition of the property adjoining the insured premises, which means the adjacent streets, alleys, etc. Injury to a resident employee when in the course of employment is also covered. This coverage refers to medical expenses, which, in the 1976 form, is defined so as to include dental work and even funeral services.

Medical payments coverage also:

- Applies to persons on the insured premises with the permission of any insured. This includes both implied permission (as in the case of a milkman or paperboy) and direct permission (a guest). It is intended that coverage for trespassers be excluded.
- Provides for injuries only if caused by accidental acts on the part of an insured, such as those occurring during sports activities, etc. The term "any insured" means persons named in the policy, relatives of any named insured, or any person under the age of twenty-one and in the care of any insured.
- Provides for employees if they are "resident employees,"

meaning persons employed in the household, like maids, gardeners, et al.

- Limits some coverage to a certain location—specifically the insured premises.

Medical payments coverage is not contingent upon demonstrable legal liability. It provides coverage for on-premises injury regardless of fault, and for away-from-the-premises injury when "caused by the activities of any insured." In cases where legal liability is proven on the part of an insured regardless of the location of the occurrence, the general liability insurance would come into play.

In Section II of the homeowners form, numerous exclusions are listed relative to both the personal liability coverages and the medical payments section. Some of the more important exclusions are as follows:

- Bodily injury or property damage is excluded where the use, loading, or unloading of aircraft or any motor vehicle is concerned, unless the vehicle involved is actually on the premises at the time the incident occurs, is not registered, and is used exclusively on the property or kept in dead storage at the residence. Coverage is also excluded when resulting from use of recreational vehicles while away from the described premises. However, this does not apply to golf carts "used for golfing purposes." It would apply to beach buggies or snowmobiles.
- Damages are not covered when involving boats owned or rented by the insured if the boat has inboard or inboard-outboard power of more than 50 horsepower, or if the boat is a sailboat more than 26 feet in length or is powered by a motor or motors producing more than 25 horsepower.
- Damages resulting from the rendering or failing to render professional services are not covered.
- Damages resulting from business pursuits are not covered. This means virtually any transaction engaged in for profit. The making of candles for sale at a craft fair would be an example.

- Damages which occur at property held by the insured for rental, other than the insured location, are not covered. (Liability protection for additional locations can be obtained through endorsements or other contracts.)
- Bodily injury or property damage which is "either expected or intended from the standpoint of the insured" is not covered. This is a broad condition, and may encompass many circumstances. If you intentionally punch someone, turn your dog loose on a belligerent mailman, or do anything else that a reasonable person would expect to cause foreseeable damage or injury, coverage will not apply.
- Also, acts done by children (who are considered insureds under the policy) expected or intended to cause damage or injury will not be covered, providing the child has reached the "age of reason" and can be seen to have an intent at all.

The standard amounts of coverage provided under Section II of the homeowner policies are inadequate in this day and age. The limits can be raised to virtually any amount you desire, and should be raised to at least $100,000. Umbrella coverages are available, increasing liability coverage to whatever level is necessary.

Umbrella Policies

An umbrella policy acts as a supplementary liability insurance policy, which can supplement not only your homeowners policy but also other policies providing liability coverage, such as an auto policy, or a policy on a piece of rental or commercial property. These policies can be bought for amounts of $1,000,000 or more. Umbrella policies typically require that a standard liability policy be carried by the policyholder, up to a certain level, ranging from $50,000 and up on homeowners policies, and from about $250,000 on auto policies. The umbrella policy is only excess insurance and does not come into play until the limits of the standard policy are exhausted.

The liability coverage provided by umbrella policies is more comprehensive than that provided by the standard homeowners policy. Umbrellas will usually cover libel, slander, false arrest, wrongful eviction, defamation of character, and invasion of privacy. When these perils are covered by the umbrella but not by the homeowners policy, they can be applied as a basic coverage with a deductible applicable.

Damage to Property of Others

This property damage coverage, provided under the "supplementary coverages" section of the Section II policy, pays for damage to or destruction of property owned by others and caused by an insured. For example, if you were to borrow your neighbor's lawnmower, and it was damaged through no fault of your own, this coverage would apply. Like the medical payments coverage, it is not contingent upon actual legal liability, but rather is intended to respond to a moral obligation. The company's limit of liability here is based on the actual cash value of the property affected, and the company has the option to repair or replace. The limit on this coverage is between $250 and $500.

This coverage excludes damage caused intentionally by an insured over the age of thirteen, property owned by or rented to an insured, or property owned by a tenant living at the insured premises. Other exclusions apply regarding rental property, business pursuits, vehicles, farm equipment, aircraft, and watercraft.

~~In the next chapter, we will look more closely at policy provisions.~~

In Sum

When you look at a policy in terms of coverage, keep in mind:

- The different kinds of property and interests covered by your policy.
- Be aware of the exclusions that apply to personal property, especially the exclusions that apply to money, jewelry, and similar property.
- Study the basic amounts of coverage—are they right for you?
- Remember supplementary or additional coverages include removal of property, debris removal, fire department service charges, reasonable repairs, plants, misuse of credit cards, forgery, and counterfeit money.
- Consider the various kinds of deductibles available, and how they work.
- Personal liability coverage applies to bodily injury or property damage for which you are legally liable.
- Remember that the medical payments to others coverage provides protection for various accidents, both on and off the insured premises.
- Become familiar with the exclusions that apply to the liability section of the homeowners policy.
- Because the standard limits for liability coverage in the homeowners policy is relatively low, additional coverage is advisable.
- The damage to property of others coverage applies to certain situations where there is no demonstrable legal liability.

5 Policy Provisions to Look For

• The Standard Fire Policy • Standard Fire Policy Provisions • The General Conditions • Provisions in Homeowners Policies

IN the previous chapter, we examined a homeowners policy closely. We looked at the various property and interests covered, and at the kinds of coverage that apply to the different categories of property insured. It is now necessary for us to look at the provisions contained in the homeowners policy, and at what a policyholder must do to conform with the requirements of the policy contract.

It is always beneficial for a policyholder to comply with policy provisions, and this is especially true when the time comes that you must file a claim. When you act in keeping with the terms of the contract, you are able to deal with the company from a position of strength. When you blatantly violate policy requirements, you compromise your position and increase the possibility of complicating your claim unnecessarily.

The 1971 version of the homeowners policies is divided into three parts, where policy provisions and requirements are set forth. The three parts are the Standard Fire Policy, the General Conditions, and the specific homeowners policy that applies. In the 1976 edition, the format is slightly different. All of the relevant provisions of the Standard Fire Policy and the General Conditions are integrated into the actual policy form. This serves to consolidate the contract into one document, and also eliminates some of the excessive wording and repeated clauses characteristic of the older format. For the most part, the provisions of the policies are the same, regardless of the form they are in. For the sake of organization, and to make matters more interesting, we will review the older format here.

The 165 lines of the Standard Fire Policy and the General Conditions are sometimes integrated into a "policy jacket," which is a folder or envelope used to contain the homeowners policy itself. This treatment of the two forms tends to downplay their importance, but they are no less a part of the contract than the homeowners policy itself.

The Standard Fire Policy

The Standard Fire Policy is the foundation of insurance policies covering real and personal property. The Standard Fire Policy may well be the most important part of any property policy, as a considerable number of requirements and provisions are contained in the form. In the early days of fire insurance, the Standard Fire Policy was frequently the only policy issued to cover a building. This is rarely the case today. The Standard Fire Policy, however, still represents the basis of modern policies. The Standard Fire Policy is a state approved form, which includes minimum coverages required by law. The policy deals with concealment and fraud, cancellation, requirements in case loss occurs, appraisal, lawsuit, as well as many other subjects, and also contains extensive conditions and exclusions.

In the 1971 homeowners form, a portion of the Standard Fire Policy is located on the front page of the policy, separated from the rest of the Standard Fire Policy. This section contains a considerable amount of relevant policy language, and essentially contains the wording that makes the Standard Fire Policy capable of standing alone as a policy contract; it is a complete insuring agreement. This section lists the term of the policy, includes the times of inception and expiration, and outlines coverage. It lists the perils insured against (fire, lightning, and removal, which are expanded by the homeowners policy). Actual cash value at the time of loss is stated as the method of valuation that applies, not exceeding the cost of replacement with like kind and quality. This section of the policy also specifies that work required by ordinance or law is not covered. This section also limits the amount of the payment to the amount of the insured's interest in the property and prohibits assignment of the policy, as well.

Standard Fire Policy Provisions

The Standard Fire Policy stipulates that the insured must be honest and accurate in representing material facts to the insurance company regarding the property covered by the policy and the policyholder's interest in that property, both at the time the policyholder applies for the insurance and after a loss has occurred. In the event of willful concealment or misrepresentation on the part of the policyholder, the entire policy becomes void. "Void" is a strong word; it means that the company can consider the policy to have never existed. Clearly, it is not wise to falsify information on an application for insurance or to misrepresent facts when filing a claim.

The Standard Fire Policy also requires that losses be reported to the company immediately. In a situation where an insured's failure to report a claim properly results in an increase in the amount of a loss, the company may not be liable to pay for all of the damage. As an example: An elderly woman residing alone returned home from shopping one evening to find her bedroom and bathroom floors covered with water, the result of a broken water-supply line. Acting in a manner she felt to be sensible and in the best interest of the insurance company, she had the bedroom and bathroom carpeting removed and placed under a patio cover to dry. She also had a carpenter nail down the floorboards when they began to warp. After checking with various retail outlets on the price of carpeting and acquiring two quotes on the floor repairs, she contacted the insurance company—more than a month after the loss occurrence.

The fact that the woman removed the carpeting and placed it on the patio to dry deprived the insurance company of the opportunity to have professional carpet cleaners attempt to salvage the carpets. As a result, the cost to the insurance company could have been several hundred dollars. Since the policyholder acted in good faith, the company might have elected to pay the claim in full, but might have considered a reduced amount, as the policyholder's actions increased the amount of the loss.

It is difficult for a company to deny a claim outright as a result of an insured's failure to report it, especially if the cost to the company has not increased as a result of the delay. If the company's rights have not been prejudiced, courts have ruled that the company must pay the claim. However, if the delay results in an aggravation of the problem and a more expensive repair, the company is not always obligated to pay the additional amount. It should also be noted that the company's liability for a loss is the cost to repair or replace at the time of the loss, irrespective of price increases which may occur between the time of the loss and the time that payment is made.

The Standard Fire Policy further stipulates that the policyholder is required to submit a "proof of loss" to the insurance company within sixty days after the date of loss. This means that it is the obligation of the insured to submit a claim indicating the amount of payment requested within sixty days. Filing proof of loss is merely an insured's formal request to the company for payment of a claim. A proof of loss must contain pertinent information regarding the insurance policy and the loss involved, and must be signed by the insured before a notary, although most companies will accept a proof of loss even though it has not been notarized. It is not necessary that the insured file formal proof of loss on a specific kind of form, although it is necessary that the proof of loss include all of the required information. You can write a proof of loss in crayon on a napkin if you want to, and it will fulfill the policy requirement, as long as the proper information is included. Most insurance companies, however, will provide policyholders with blank proof of loss forms when requested to do so. A proof of loss must include:

- The time and cause of the loss.
- The interest of the insured and all other parties in the property.
- Information about all other insurance covering the property, or a statement that no other insurance applies if that is true.
- Information about changes in the title to the property, or the occupancy or use of the property.
- Information about all encumbrances on the property.
- The actual cash value of the property insured at the time of loss.
- Proofs of loss must be signed and notarized by all named insureds.
- Repair estimates, plans, specifications, inventories, and supporting documentation will also constitute part of a proof of loss if submitted along with the other required information.

The sixty-day period for filing proof of loss can be extended by the company in writing, and usually is in cases where the policyholder is cooperative and is making an honest effort to get a claim in order. Insurance companies frequently notify policyholders of the sixty-day requirement for filing proof of loss in writing, as the company cannot expect policyholders to be aware of the provision. If the company fails to notify the insured of this requirement, the company usually waives its right to require a proof of loss within sixty days.

As an example: A disorganized policyholder is burglarized and reports the incident two days after the loss. The company requests that an inventory of stolen items be completed by the insured and submitted to it. Twenty months later, the insured submits a demand for several thousand dollars. The company might take the position that the insured violated the provision of the policy by failing to file formal claim within sixty days, and might attempt to settle the claim based upon a compromise. If the insured were to hold out for full payment, the company would probably decide to honor the claim as submitted, since the policyholder reported the loss immediately but was never notified in writing of the sixty-day deadline for filing his claim. The company would waive its right to require that the claim be submitted within sixty days.

If an insurance company notifies you of the sixty-day requirement for filing formal claim and you fail to submit a claim within that time, the company would probably remain obligated to honor the claim. It would, however, not be obligated to respond to damages that had been aggravated by your delay in filing the claim. The company would most likely contend that your procrastination increased the amount of the loss, and would reduce the amount of the claim by an appropriate sum. In some circumstances the company might be in a position to deny your claim altogether as a result of your failure to comply with the provisions of the policy contract.

When you file proof of loss, you obligate the company to act. It must accept the proof of loss and pay the claim, or reject the proof of loss within a period of time regulated by state law, usually between thirty and sixty days. If you do go to the extent of filing a proof of loss, be sure to provide sufficient documentation to substantiate your claim. In difficult circumstances, it may be effective to file proof of loss merely to elicit a response to your demands. However, in most cases where a proof of loss is required and an agreement has been reached, the representative will fill out the form and mail it to you to be signed and notarized. Only in rare circumstances will a company insist that a policyholder submit a proof of loss without first having sent the insured a completed form.

If you sign a proof of loss and settle with the company on an amount of money for a claim, the settlement amount and proof of loss apply only to the damage discovered at the time the document is signed. It does not relieve the company of liability for damage or loss discovered after that time. As an illustration, assume that you were to settle a claim for a water-stained table based on the cost to refinish the top, and later discovered stains on the legs of the table. The company would remain liable to you for the cost of refinishing the table legs.

The Standard Fire Policy outlines the insured's responsibilities in case of a loss as follows:

- Protecting the damaged property from further damage. (This includes boarding up or covering holes in the structure to protect against damage by weather, protecting exposed property from theft, vandalism, etc.)
- Giving immediate written notice to the company of any loss. (Written notice to the agent is good enough, and a telephone call to the agent is also generally considered sufficient to comprise notice to the company of a loss.)
- Separating the damaged and undamaged property.
- Providing the company with a complete inventory of the destroyed, damaged, and undamaged property, giving in detail quantities, costs (replacement costs), actual cash value (replacement cost less depreciation), and amount claimed. This is your determination of the amount of the claim. Remember, the company does not have to pay your claim amount automatically.

- Placing all damaged property in the best possible order.
- Submitting a proof of loss to the company within sixty days after the loss occurs.
- Submission to examination under oath.
- Making available to company representatives all that remains of any damaged or destroyed property. This means that the company has the right to examine damaged property as many times as desired.
- Submission to the company of any bills and invoices available to substantiate ownership, purchase price, or value.

The General Conditions

The General Conditions section of the policy outlines several policy provisions and requirements, and also contains various conditions and exclusions. This section pertains to a wide variety of issues that involve both the property and liability sections of the policy. Information contained in the General Conditions is important, and should be reviewed carefully.

The General Conditions give the policyholder the right to make temporary or permanent repairs to the insured property following a loss, but only to the extent that they are necessary to protect the property from further damage. The insured does not have the right to repair damages prior to inspection of the affected property by a company representative. Clearly, such an action would prejudice the rights of the company, as the company would have no way of knowing whether the work completed was actually necessary. Also, the General Conditions stipulate that the insured is required to retain bills and invoices documenting moneys spent in completing emergency repairs. In the 1976 form, not only is coverage specifically included for emergency repairs, but the policy language actually requires the policyholder to make repairs to protect the property, and to keep records of the costs.

Listed below are some other notable provisions and requirements outlined in the General Conditions section of the policy:

- Relative to theft claims, the homeowners policies are always secondary to any policies that would apply in their absence, such as insurance on luggage purchased through a travel agency, etc.
- "Insured" means the person or persons named on the policy, and includes the spouse and relatives of the policyholder and any other person under the age of twenty-one in the care of any insured, if they are residents of the policyholder's household.
- The insured has liability protection at temporary residences.
- In the event of loss of one item of a pair or set (vases, end tables, etc.), the company is liable for the damaged item only or the difference in the value of the set before and after the loss, but not for the entire set.
- In case of a loss, the insured must protect the property from further damage.
- The 1971 homeowners edition states that other insurance on the property covering like perils is not permitted. This provision is not in the new form. Other insurance is allowed, and the company is liable only for its prorated share of a loss.
- When an event occurs that will result in a claim under the personal liability or medical payments coverage, the insured must notify the company "as soon as practical."
- The insured must cooperate with the company in any liability claim.

Provisions in Homeowners Policies

The sections of the homeowners policies derived from the actual policy forms, as opposed to the Standard Fire Policy and the General Conditions, also contain policy provisions, although most of the provisions come from the Standard Fire

Policy and General Conditions portion of the contract. The homeowners policy forms, exclusive of the Standard Fire Policy and General Conditions, follow a standard format, consisting of four sections: the "deck page" (which contains amounts of coverages, inception and expiration dates, the address of the insured premises, and other technical data); a "description of property covered" section (which specifies the kind of property covered, i.e., dwellings, personal property, etc.); the "insuring agreement" (which outlines the nature of the coverage provided by the policy, i.e., all risk, named peril, etc.), and a conditions and exclusions section.

The homeowners policies require that theft claims be reported to the police immediately. It is wise to provide police with a complete list of items stolen at the time the initial police report is made, if at all possible. Some insurance companies require that the police report list all items that are included in the inventory submitted to the company. When the police report inventory is incomplete, some companies insist that the policyholder file a supplemental report, which is invariably a time-consuming task. It frequently takes two weeks or longer for a company to secure a police report, and in cases where a supplemental report must be filed by the policyholder and obtained by the company, the delay can be a month or more. It is often difficult for a policyholder to provide police with a complete inventory of stolen property initially, since stolen items are frequently discovered missing days after a burglary, and because victims are usually emotionally distraught immediately following a burglary. However, if possible, be complete in reporting items stolen to the police.

It is always the insured's responsibility to prove that a loss has been sustained; it is not the company's responsibility to prove that the insured has *not* sustained a loss. This principle is not stipulated in insurance policies, but is nonetheless accepted by the insurance industry and the courts, and is in effect an unwritten policy requirement.

In some situations, an insurance company is obligated to

accept a policyholder's word, even though it is difficult for a policyholder to demonstrate a loss. This is true when questions arise regarding the facts surrounding a loss. The circumstances of the loss of an article (which may mean the difference between a theft claim or a mysterious disappearance claim) or questions regarding ownership of items included in a claim are examples. In such cases, the company must usually accept a policyholder's version of the facts, unless the company is able to obtain conflicting evidence. If a policyholder continues to assume a position based on the misrepresentation of facts, and an insurance company is able to produce solid evidence of misrepresentation, the insured is guilty of fraud.

In dealing with concrete issues, however, it is always the policyholder's obligation to demonstrate a loss. If a policyholder contends that a stolen watch was worth $700, the company has the right to require that the value be proved. The same goes for damage to a building. The company has the right to require that the insured document that the amount claimed is based on an appropriate cost to repair.

An insurance company must typically accept an insured's viewpoint in determining whether a certain condition existed before a loss occurred, or was a result of the loss. For example: A water supply line in your bathroom breaks, and the room is flooded. The vinyl flooring bubbles and separates from the subfloor, so you file a claim. Let us further assume you have hardwood flooring beneath the vinyl floor. The company representative inspects the damage a week after it happened, notices the floorboards are warped, and asks if they were warped before the incident. Essentially, the representative has to accept your answer in good faith, or prove otherwise, at the company's cost. It is reasonable to assume that the floorboards were warped by the exposure to water, and if you inform the representative that the floor was level before the loss, the representative cannot arbitrarily take the position that you are lying, and refuse to pay for repairs to the wood floor. By contrast, if the representative can demonstrate that the floorboards were warped before the loss occurrence, you would be guilty of misrepresenting facts to the insurer.

There are no set rules governing when the company must accept your word and when you must prove your loss. Generally, if it is possible for you to demonstrate a concrete issue (the value of an item or the cost of a repair), you can rightfully be required to do so. If there is a question regarding the general facts surrounding a loss which you cannot reasonably be expected to substantiate (such as the amount of loose change contained in a jar on your dresser prior to a burglary), it is felt that the company is obligated to accept your version of the facts in good faith. If you are willing to obtain signed affidavits documenting your side of the story (when no other method of proving your loss is practical), you are doing everything possible to demonstrate your loss, and the company owes you a reasonable settlement.

Assume that you purchase a stereo system from a friend for cash, that no bill of sale changes hands when the deal is made, and that your friend moves to Guam immediately following the transaction. If the stereo system was stolen and included as part of an insurance claim, the insurance company representative might be inclined to request that supporting papers be submitted to substantiate the value of the stereo and the fact that you actually owned it. The circumstances surrounding your acquisition of the stereo might lead him to believe that you never actually owned it. In such a case, it is felt that it is the representative's obligation to accept your contention and to compensate you based upon the full value of the stereo, especially if you obtained signed affidavits from your friends and neighbors indicating that they had seen the stereo in your home.

It is always the obligation of the insured to assume the financial burden of demonstrating a loss. Say you place a newspaper in your oven to dry, and end up with a small fire in your oven. If you suspect that the oven is damaged and should be checked, you must absorb the cost of the service call. The company only owes you the cost to repair the oven, if it is damaged. Also, if a contractor charges a fee to write an estimate, you must pay it, unless the company volunteers to do so.

In situations where it is clearly conceivable for you to prove your loss, and you do so to a reasonable degree, the burden to dispute your figures falls on the company. Let us say your house is damaged by a falling piece of Skylab. You obtain two itemized and detailed estimates, both of which include only work necessitated by the loss. If the company feels your claim is unreasonable and takes the position that your figures are inordinately high, it becomes the company's obligation to prove that you are asking for too much. The initial burden of proof is on you, but once you present your claim, the burden to demonstrate that your claim is unreasonable falls on the company. The cost to dispute claims is often high, and most companies will take measures to settle claims, rather than hire contractors to dispute inflated bids or argue for weeks on end over a few dollars.

In Sum

When studying policy provisions to look for, keep in mind:

- It is always to your benefit to act in keeping with policy provisions.
- Most policy provisions are derived from the Standard Fire Policy, which is the foundation of policies insuring property.
- The policyholder must be honest in reporting material facts to the insurer.
- Losses must be reported to the company immediately.
- The policyholder must submit a formal claim, in the form of a "proof of loss," to the company within sixty days of the date of loss.
- The Standard Fire Policy outlines the insured's responsibilities after a loss.
- Several policy provisions are derived from the General Conditions.
- The policyholder has the right to make temporary repairs to the premises following a loss.

- The homeowners policies require that theft claims be reported to the police immediately.
- It is always the policyholder's responsibility to prove that a loss has been sustained.
- It is always the policyholder's obligation to assume the financial burden of proving a loss.

# 6 Floater Policies

• Personal Articles Floater • Personal Property Floater • Computer Insurance • Are Floaters Necessary? • Putting a Value on Your Property • Obtaining Appraisals • Choosing an Appraiser • Appraising an Appraiser

IN addition to the standard homeowners policies, insurance companies also offer "floater policies." Floaters are simply separate insurance policies written to cover specific items. The basic homeowners policy covers personal property in general, called "unscheduled" personal property. This coverage, as you have seen, is subject to exclusions and limitations. In many cases, personal property insured under floater policies is "scheduled," meaning that the property is listed and described separately in a schedule of items. Floater policies can be endorsements to your homeowners policy, or separate policies entirely. Either way, the coverage is not a duplication of the homeowners policy: the floater is the only policy that applies to the scheduled items.

The name of this kind of policy has come from marine insurance. In the early days of insurance, goods transported by land were insured under policies which came to be known as "inland marine" policies, called "floaters." The term was later extended to refer to all such policies written on specific property.

Personal property insured under floater policies is usually covered on an all risk basis, and this coverage is all risk in a very real way. The coverage provided is extensive. The limitations applicable to personal property listed in the standard homeowners policy do not apply to items scheduled in a floater. Although the all risk coverage provided under floater policies is extremely broad, most floater policies exclude damages resulting from wear and tear, insects, vermin, inherent vice, acts of war, nuclear reactions, government regulations, and confiscation by authorities. The exclusions differ slightly between policies, and it is wise to become familiar with the exclusions notable in the policies you purchase.

The coverage provided under floater policies is so extensive that companies can be obligated to pay for repairs even when the item in question has not sustained any damage per se. As an example: Imagine that a policyholder travels extensively throughout Europe, and, naturally, takes his expensive camera equipment along. Upon his return home, he discovers that the camera is not functioning properly. He determines that the relatively new camera has not been damaged in any direct way, but that, in his opinion, the debilitated condition of the instrument is the result of its having been jarred during his excursion. Although some natural jarring could not actually be construed as damage, the insurance company might pay to have the camera repaired. Most likely the company would reason that the camera was operating correctly when the insured left on his trip, so it must have been "damaged" during the excursion, although no one could say exactly how.

Personal Articles Floater

The most common policy used to insure personal property is the "personal articles floater." This policy is designed to cover nine different classes of property. These include: jewelry, furs, cameras (and related equipment), musical instruments, silverware, golfers' equipment, fine arts, stamps, and coins. A specific amount of insurance is listed for each item, and a separate premium is charged. There are some minor limitations that apply, one of which is that fine arts must be at a location specified in the policy.

Newly acquired jewelry, furs, cameras, and musical instruments are covered automatically for 25 percent of the amount of insurance for the class of property involved or $10,000, whichever is less. You must report the new acquisition to the company within thirty days and pay the additional premium from the date that the property was acquired. Newly acquired fine arts are covered for actual cash value, limited to 25 percent of the limit on fine arts. You must report the new property to the company within ninety days and, again, pay the additional premium charged from the date of acquisition.

Fine arts, such as antique furniture or paintings, are not covered for loss caused by repairing, restoring, or retouching, or by breakage of certain fragile and glass items, unless caused by fire or lightning, explosion, aircraft and vehicles, windstorm, earthquake, flood, vandalism, or derailment or overturn of a conveyance. Property on exhibit is not covered unless the location is listed in the policy.

Other exclusions apply to stamps and coins, including fading, scratching, damage from handling, property shipped by certain means, and the like. There are also other special provisions that apply to fine arts, golfers' equipment, stamps, and coins.

The amount payable under the personal articles floater varies among the categories of property included. In some cases, the payment is based upon the amount of insurance that applies, which is seen to be the value of the item, and is paid automatically in the case of a total loss. On some property, the payment will depend on the market value of the items involved at the time of loss, and may be subject to a maximum limit per collection or individual item. On still other property, the company's liability is limited to the lowest of four amounts:

- the actual cash value of the property at the time of loss
- the cost to repair or restore the property
- the cost of replacement
- the amount of insurance

There is also a "pair and set" clause in the personal articles floater, which gives the company the right to repair or replace the item damaged or to pay the difference between the value of the entire set before the loss and the remaining portion of the set.

In sum, the personal articles floater is a rather complex policy, and it is prudent to review the provisions that apply to the property you insure under it.

Some companies offer endorsements to the standard homeowners policy that eliminate the need for floater policies in some cases. The endorsements serve to raise the limits on certain kinds of property, such as furs or jewelry, that are subject to a limit in the standard homeowners policy. For example, the limits on jewelry can be raised from $500 to $2,500 by endorsement. This approach is generally less expensive than insuring property under a floater policy. It might be a good idea to insure smaller and less valuable jewelry items under such an endorsement, and use the floater to cover more valuable pieces. As pointed out, not every company offers this option, and you may have to seek out a company that offers such insurance.

Personal Property Floater

There is also a "personal property floater," which is used to insure specific categories of property, such as clothing, silverware, sporting equipment, etc. This form is usually used in the absence of a standard homeowners policy, when coverage is desired for specific kinds of property, such as a golf pro's clubs and other equipment. This form will also provide coverage for personal property on a blanket basis (meaning that all personal property is insured for a given amount, much as is the case with a tenant's homeowners policy), except that the additional coverages provided by a homeowners policy, such as liability coverage and additional living expenses coverages, are not included.

Computer Insurance

With the ever-growing number of persons who now own computers you may wonder how computers are covered.

Coverage for computer equipment depends upon whether the equipment is considered business or personal property, and on the coverage provided for such property under the specific policy that applies.

If computer equipment is strictly personal property, then it is covered for the same perils as all other types of personal property. If the equipment is strictly business property, all of the policy provisions that apply to business property will apply. If the equipment is used both for business and personal purposes, then it can be covered as personal property, for this coverage is usually more extensive than that provided for business property.

Under the 1971 policies, business personal property away from the premises is excluded from coverage, so under this form a computer away from the premises would not be covered, while one on the premises would. The coverage under the 1976 policies is the same, except that they also exclude business property pertaining to a business conducted on the premises. For example, if you were to use a computer for a mail order business conducted from your home, it would not be covered under the 1976 homeowners policies.

For more comprehensive coverage to computer equipment, the HO–5 policy or an endorsement to an HO–3 that adds all risk coverage to personal property would be a good choice. You can also insure computers under a business property policy if the equipment is used in a business. But the best coverage for your computer is under a floater policy.

Are Floaters Necessary?

Given that there are approximately four million burglaries in the United States each year, we can safely assume that it is prudent to insure valuable personal property in most cases. Furthermore, with recent economic fluctuations, the standard limits of the homeowners policies on jewelry and other valuables do not provide much real protection. The question of whether or not floaters are necessary for you is best addressed in view of your unique needs. Essentially, there are two reasons to insure property under a floater policy. The first is to obtain a greater amount of coverage. For example, we have seen that in the standard homeowners policy, jewelry coverage is limited to $500 for loss by theft. If the jewelry is scheduled, the amount can be raised to any level desired. The second reason is to obtain more comprehensive coverage for certain property. The policyholder mentioned in the earlier example obtained highly comprehensive all risk coverage for his camera equipment by scheduling it.

Buying floater policies is the only way to *fully* insure property that is subject to limitations in the homeowners policy. Most people have some form of property that they would do well to insure under a floater policy. Many kinds of collections are obvious examples, especially if they fall into the categories of property subject to limitations: coin and stamp collections and antique silverware are two that come to mind. Other collectibles that are not subject to coverage limitations under the standard homeowners forms are also prime candidates for scheduling. If a large and valuable gun collection were stolen, for example, the homeowners policy would only pay actual cash value, even if there was no limitation on the property. Other valuables, such as antique furniture and paintings, are likewise not subject to limitations, but are subject to certain kinds of damage that might not be covered under the standard homeowners policy, such as breakage or staining. Also, getting paid on a claim involving this kind of property might be easier if there were appraisals available to substantiate value.

There are, of course, options to protecting your personal property with floaters or endorsements. The most obvious is to take your chances and leave the property uninsured. However, the loss of a cache of heirloom jewelry representing an entire family history can cause a tremendous amount of needless heartbreak, and for this reason alone simply leaving property uninsured may not be a satisfactory alternative. Another option is to take the steps available to protect your property to the best of your ability, which might involve hiding it or placing it in a safe embedded in the foundation of your house. There are dangers here as well. Keep in mind that housekeepers, repair personnel, decorators, or friends may discover your hiding place, and may disclose the location, unknowingly or otherwise, to the wrong person. I was once at a party where a woman I know well and respect told a small room full of people about a neighbor who had $60,000 worth of gold in his basement. I hope the information did not fall on the wrong ears.

Still another alternative is the safe deposit box. The obvious disadvantage to keeping valuable property in a safe deposit box is that it is not available for your use. And there are other things to consider about this alternative. Contrary to popular belief, safe deposit boxes are not completely secure. There have been many instances of thieves stealing property contained in them. Also, in some states, the bank can open your box and sell the contents if you forget or neglect to pay the rental fee.

Property contained in safe deposit boxes is not insured by the bank. However, in-vault coverage is available for personal property, through your insurance broker or agent. The fee is nominal, in the neighborhood of a few cents per $100 worth of jewelry, for example. Your agent or broker can bind coverage for the property when out of the box with a mere phone call, and will bill you for the coverage provided during the time that the property is not in the bank vault. This approach is something of a hassle, and perhaps the best thing to do is to just pay the premium and insure the property if you plan to use it frequently.

Putting a Value on Your Property

Determining the value of property to be insured under floater policies is the job of the policyholder. There are several things to consider when valuing property for coverage under a floater. Under most floater policies, the amount of insurance is the maximum amount that the company will ever be liable to pay in the event of a loss. In most cases, if the company can replace the property for less than the amount of the policy, it has the option of doing so, and it keeps the savings. The company is obligated to pay the stated value or the replacement cost, whichever is less. (In rare cases, floater policies will stipulate valuation at actual cash value instead of replacement cost. This should be allowed only if it is what you want.) If your wedding ring is scheduled for $3,000, and the company can replace it for $2,000, that may be the amount of payment if it is lost or stolen. Under this kind of policy, the importance of correct valuation is clear. If the company replaces the property involved for an amount considerably less than the amount of insurance, then the premium paid has been too high all along.

Keep in mind that the company may have many avenues available for replacement of property. It may deal with a firm that specializes in replacing property for insurance companies, and may realize discounts that are not available to the general public. It may also purchase items through dealers or at auction. The cost of the item in question at retail may not always be the amount paid on a claim.

One way to combat this problem is to purchase an agreed value policy, or a valued contract. These policies stipulate a value that is accepted by the company to be the agreed value of the item, and in the case of a total loss, that amount is paid without question. Other considerations that might arise with the standard type of floater, such as retail or replacement cost, fluctuations in value, and the like, are not relevant to payment of the claim. This kind of policy may be slightly diffi-cult to obtain, and in some cases may cost more, but might be worth it if the item insured is of great importance to you.

There are two schools of thought about deciding upon the value of your scheduled property. Some say the wisest route is to insure the property for a relatively low value and base the amount of insurance on actual cash value. This means that you would only be paid actual cash value in case of a loss. If you were to have an expensive violin stolen, for example, you would have to shop around for a used one or buy one on sale in order to replace the item with the amount of the payment from the insurance company. This is practical in many instances, however, for you will certainly save money on your floater policy by using a low value figure as the basis for the amount of insurance.

If you do not want to go the low value route, and you

insure your property for full replacement cost, be sure that your value figures are up to date. In this time of economic fluctuation, the value of gold, silver, precious stones, and the like change tremendously in relatively short periods of time. It is a good idea to review your coverages at least once a year to make sure that they are in line with current values.

In sum, the method of valuation that you use in insuring your property under floater policies should be influenced by your specific needs and desires. An expensive stereo system might be insured for actual cash value, if you want to keep the cost of the insurance down and are willing to search around for used replacement items after a loss. If used replacements would not be acceptable to you, then valuation should be at replacement cost.

Obtaining Appraisals

The first step in obtaining appraisals is finding out what the insurance company requires in order to insure your property under a floater policy. At times, a company will use a bill of sale or a catalog price to set the value of an item for a floater policy. A verbal quote from a knowledgeable source may even be sufficient. If such a method of operation serves your purposes, and you know that the figure is correct, this approach is completely acceptable. If the insurance company is not content to use a bill of sale, catalog price, or your good word to establish value, you will need to get an appraisal of some kind.

There are two kinds of appraisals: formal appraisals, which are usually written in triplicate, elaborately bound, and expensive; and letter appraisals, which are single pages describing the item or items to be insured, and indicating the appraised values that apply. If you have a large number of items to appraise, or if the items to be insured are of extremely high value, a formal appraisal might make sense. Such appraisals are typically prohibitively expensive for the average policyholder, and simply are not necessary for insurance purposes. Letter appraisals will suffice for most insurance applications, whether for a single item, a schedule of jewelry, or a hodge-podge of various things. Letter appraisals from a typical art or jewelry dealer might cost as little as $20 in some cases, and should not exceed $200 in any case.

Choosing an Appraiser

None of the fifty states require that personal property appraisers be licensed. This means that you may have to check to see that an appraiser you select is reputable and qualified to work for you. Your insurance agent or broker is an obvious source of information here. Agents and brokers see a considerable number of appraisals from different appraisers in their area. Lawyers and bank personnel who are involved in estate dissolution may also have ideas about a good appraiser. Museums and historical societies frequently have information about qualified appraisers, especially if the items to be appraised are of the kind with which the museum deals. Friends and neighbors are also sources of information about qualified appraisers in your area.

In essence, there are two kinds of personal property appraisers. There are general appraisers, who deal with many different kinds of property. This kind of appraiser is typically involved in assessing the value of property included in an estate, as well as in insurance claims. And then there are specialists, who specialize in and appraise only one kind of property. This might include an art dealer who appraises only art items, or a jeweler who will appraise jewelry. If you have many items of a varied nature to have appraised, you may well benefit from the services of a general appraiser. If the items you intend to insure are of a singular and specialized nature, the specialist is the obvious choice for you.

In most instances, a specialist is the best choice for the aver age person, since few among us have a house full of widely varied museum pieces. Most of us have a few jewelry items, an antique item or two, or a stamp collection that should be scheduled.

When looking for a specialist, it is usually wise to start with the people you know. If you know a jeweler, art dealer, or furrier in your area, and have had satisfactory dealings with them in the past, see if they do appraisals. If not, they may be able to refer you to someone they know who will fit the bill. As mentioned previously, you can also contact museums that deal with the kind of property you want to have appraised. And then there is always the Yellow Pages. The problem here, of course, is that you may know little or nothing about the appraisers listed. There are, however, ways to gain some insight into an individual's or firm's capabilities.

If it is a general appraiser that you need, you will probably select your appraiser from one of three groups: professional appraisers, auction companies, and appraisal companies. Which appraiser you use will depend on your individual needs.

Auction house personnel generally gain their knowledge about the value of personal property by selling such property at auction. In doing so, they see a considerable amount of merchandise. Keep in mind that the price that an item brings at auction is an actual cash value amount, and sometimes a relatively low one at that. The price that something would bring at auction is a fair indication of its market value, however, and might be an appropriate basis for an insurance appraisal if that is the kind of value figure that you want.

There are several large auction houses, among them Christie's, with offices in New York City and Beverly Hills, and Sotheby, with offices in New York City, Boston, Philadelphia, Palm Beach, Chicago, Washington, D.C., Houston, San Francisco, and Los Angeles. There are also many smaller and local auction companies that you will find listed under "Auctioneers" or "Appraisers" in the Yellow Pages. Large metropolitan areas tend to have the biggest and best auction houses, and you may have to travel some distance to find one.

Auction companies will do appraisals at your home, in their facility, or, at times, based only on a photograph. If the auction firm sends an appraiser to your house to do a formal appraisal, be prepared for a hefty bill. The cost can well reach $1,000 per day, with travel expenses tacked on in addition. There may also be a relatively high minimum charge, perhaps $500 or more. It always makes sense to take the items to be appraised to the appraiser or auction company, unless your time is worth more than theirs. Letter appraisals are also available from auction companies and at reasonable rates in most cases.

Some auction companies will actually provide free appraisals by mail if you send them a photograph of the item to be appraised. These appraisals are typically qualified by the auction company, and are not usually accepted by insurance companies. Everyone knows that a sound appraisal cannot be done from a photograph, and ultimately such an appraisal may be worth precisely what it cost. However, it will be one more indication of value available to you, and can be used as a check against a letter appraisal that you paid for. It might also be worthwhile in determining if something is valuable enough to schedule, or if an item has value that you were not aware of. For instance, if you think that your aunt's trunk in the attic may be a valuable antique, this might be a good way to find out. Although verbal appraisals are not acceptable for establishing value to your insurance company, they can serve as a touchstone, or might assist you in determining whether or not something should be separately insured.

Professional appraisers are also an available option. There are many individuals and firms operating as appraisers, both general and specialists. Appraisal companies are an option as well. These firms typically are involved in the appraisal of business and industrial property, although some work with personal property as well.

Appraising an Appraiser

If you know and trust the appraiser you are going to work with, you are a member of a fortunate minority. If you are in the more common position of dealing with an appraiser whose reputation is largely unknown to you, or if you merely want to check into the reputation and capability of an appraiser who has come highly recommended, there are many ways to determine if a specific appraiser is competent and right for you.

If you are considering dealing with a shop or gallery, examine the items sold there. Check to see if the dealer sells items similar to those that you are going to have appraised. If you are dealing with an art gallery, for example, see if the dealer sells the kind of art you are going to insure, and from the same period. A dealer specializing in modern art will probably not be the right person to appraise your Rembrandt. The same is true with a jeweler. See if the items sold are of the same type and price range as yours. Talk to the dealer. You should be able to get an idea of the dealer's areas of expertise merely by asking about them. A reputable dealer or retailer will tell you if he or she is not qualified to appraise a certain piece of property.

Ask about the education of the appraiser. See if there has been any formal education at specialized schools such as the Gemological Institute of America. Ask for references. See if the appraiser's customers have been satisfied with the services provided. Call the Better Business Bureau in your area and see if any complaints have been filed against the firm or individual you are considering using. If there have been, find out if they were resolved satisfactorily. Review the product: you should be able to see a sample appraisal if you ask to. Find out if the appraiser offers an update service. This will not only provide an indication of the appraiser's commitment to the field, but is also a valuable service to you. The cost of an update, completed every two or three years, should be moderate.

Membership in professional organizations is an indication of experience and expertise. Two of the larger organizations are the American Society of Appraisers (ASA) and the Appraisers Association of America (AAA). The ASA includes industrial and real estate appraisers, as well as personal property appraisers. There are three levels of membership, senior, member, and associate, and the level one holds depends on experience. A senior must have been a full-time appraiser for five years, and a member, two years. Both must pass qualifying examinations. An associate is considered a trainee, at an entry-level position. The association provides a directory of seniors and members who handle personal property appraisals, which is available by sending a legal-size envelope with postage for two ounces to: ASA, Dulles International Airport, P.O. Box 17265, Washington, D.C. 20041.

Members in the Appraisers Association of America are typically fine arts appraisers. Each must have five years' experience as a full-time appraiser to qualify for membership. Each member must also submit references and copies of their work to the association before being admitted. The AAA also has a directory available for a nominal fee. The address is Appraisers Association of America, 60 East 42nd Street, New York, New York 10017.

Some stamp dealers and experts may be members of the Professional Numismatists Guild, which requires five years' full-time experience in the field to qualify for membership. The American Stamp Dealers Association requires only two years' experience. Antique book dealers may be members of the Antiquarian Book Sellers Association, which requires three years' experience and two member-sponsors for each applicant.

There are certain things that characterize a sound, proper appraisal. The appraisal should always be on the appraiser's letterhead, and should be dated. It should be as detailed as possible. Most appraisals are done in duplicate or triplicate. Two copies are all you need: one for you and one for the insurance company. The appraiser may keep the third copy. Appraisals should always include retail prices, and not wholesale or discount prices. Even if you paid a discount price for the property, the appraisal should still be based on the retail cost.

A jewelry appraisal should note the size and number of stones, and mention their color, cut, clarity, and quality. The setting should be described in detail, with the type and grade of metal included. An appraisal of silver flatware should include the name of the manufacturer and the pattern, the weight, and the kind and number of pieces. Any distinguishing characteristics, such as monograms or makers' marks, should be noted.

An antique or fine arts appraisal should include a good description of the item, including size, materials, colors, and distinguishing qualities, as well as the name of the artist or maker. Separate values should be noted for each item included in the appraisal. If available, historical facts about the item should be included, such as past ownership and exhibits and publications the item has been in.

All appraisers charge a fee for their services, and the basis for the fee should always be agreed upon before the appraisal is prepared. Fees are based on either a flat fee per item, an hourly rate, or a percentage of the appraised value of the property involved. Flat fees range from as low as $10 per item to as much as $100 or so. Hourly rates vary as well, from $20 per hour to $150 or more. Again, expenses for travel and the like might be added to the cost. Percentage fees usually range from 1 to 2 percent of the value of the property appraised.

It is felt by many appraisers that charging a percentage fee is unethical, as it presents an obvious conflict of interest: the more the item is appraised for, the more the appraiser makes on the deal. Indeed, there have been instances where appraisals prepared on such a basis proved to be inflated, with the appraiser's monetary gain cited as the reason. The American Society of Appraisers considers the charging of percentage fees grounds for expulsion. Always be sure to tell an appraiser that you want the appraisal for insurance purposes. Be sure the appraiser knows that the property is not for sale. Some appraisers are inclined to minimize appraisals in order to have the opportunity to buy the property at a bargain price.

Do not use estate appraisals for insurance purposes, unless you are looking for a very conservative figure. An estate sale is something of a forced-sale situation, and the prices that items bring are usually below market to some extent.

In Sum

When studying and shopping for floater policies, keep in mind:

- The all risk coverage provided by some floaters is extremely extensive, and highly valuable.
- The most common policy used to insure personal property is the "personal articles floater," which is designed to cover nine different classes of property.
- Floater policies contain exclusions, and you should become familiar with the exclusions in your own policies.
- It is possible to insure personal property with endorsements to the homeowners policy, thus eliminating the need for a floater. This can be an advantageous course of action in some cases.
- The question of whether or not you need floater policies should be decided by your own unique needs.
- There are two reasons to insure property under a floater policy: to obtain a greater amount of insurance on the property and to obtain more comprehensive coverage.
- There are options to insuring property under floaters, and some of them can be useful.

- Putting a value on your property is an important part of insuring property under a floater policy.
- Obtaining value figures and choosing an appraiser are aspects of insuring property under floaters that warrant careful consideration.
- Do not use estate appraisals for insurance purposes, because you will get a figure that is on the low side.

7 When You Have to File a Claim

*• The Policyholder's Position • The Insurance
Company Position • Questionable Practices • The
Elements of a Valid Claim • Consequential
Losses • Negotiating a Settlement*

The Policyholder's Position

If you ever find yourself in a situation that requires filing an
insurance claim, you will quickly realize that the world of policy
contracts and claims handling is a confusing and complex one.
You may also become aware that you will be operating at a
serious disadvantage unless you know enough to monitor the
details of filing a claim and to protect your interests successfully.
Advertisers and insurance salespeople frequently imply that
filing a claim is an effortless and satisfactory experience. In
fact, it is usually somewhat difficult, and can be more like a
tax audit than anything else. Your initial inclination may be
to rely on your insurance agent for assistance, but you will

probably discover that most insurance salespeople have a limited knowledge of claims processing.

By approaching an insurance claim with a pragmatic attitude, creative common sense, and a willingness to become involved in the situation, it is possible for a policyholder to affect the outcome of a claim a great deal. And in fact, the varied circumstances of property losses frequently place policyholders in a position that is less than ideal, one where a creative approach to a claim may be necessary if the policyholder is to come through the ordeal with the feeling that the outcome is acceptable.

Certain approaches to claims intended to improve the overall outcome for a policyholder are perfectly sound, legal, and right. Others might not be. Sometimes there is a temptation to manipulate things in a way that is less than scrupulous, and even to fabricate details in order to insure a favorable end result. We all know that a knowledge of insurance can be used to perpetrate fraudulent claims. Unfortunately, the field of insurance is one where the dishonest side of human nature is apt to be seen, where the temptation to lie a little bit may be too hard for some to resist. Beyond what effect this dishonesty might have on us as a collective society, there is a definite price to be paid. An increase in the cost of insurance is passed on to all of us.

It is a common opinion that insurance companies have the deck stacked heavily in their favor where claims are concerned; actually, the opposite is true. It is the policyholder who is in the most favorable position. Insurance policies are not ultimately interpreted by policyholders, company claims people, or attorneys. They are interpreted by courts of law. As questions regarding policy interpretation are brought before the courts, the decisions handed down by the courts become case law. Insurance companies must act in ways consistent with case law in processing claims. To do otherwise can constitute an unfair claims settlement practice or bad faith.

Courts consistently extend the benefit of all doubts to policy-holders. If a case involves a claim which cannot be fully substantiated by an insured, a court will usually rule in favor of the policyholder and require that the company pay the claim. At times, courts do decide in favor of the company when the insured holds a position that is clearly wrong and unreasonable. However, questionable cases are resolved in favor of the policy-holder in most cases, and it is the insurance company that is the underdog in the courtroom.

In certain instances, courts have held that a policyholder cannot be bound by the provisions of the policy unless notified of the provisions by the company in writing. Companies are frequently required to pay claims even after policy provisions have been blatantly violated by the policyholder. As mentioned in chapter 5, although a policy may require that claims be reported to the company immediately following a loss, a company cannot deny a claim because of late reporting as long as the company's rights are not prejudiced by the late reporting.

The overall effect of court decisions has been to broaden the coverage provided by insurance policies considerably. This is true to such an extent that at this time, insurance companies are sometimes required to pay for things that are specifically excluded in the homeowners policy. An example of this is that some companies are now paying for damages caused by earthquake, even though this cause of loss is excluded. This issue is explored in greater detail in chapter 12, which deals with policy interpretation.

Companies are not only required to act in keeping with court precedents, but they can also be required to follow certain standard practices that have become universally accepted by the insurance industry in general. To do otherwise might cause a court to frown on their actions if a sticky case ever got to trial, and might even be seen as bad faith. An example of a standard practice is the requirement that companies issue advance additional living expense payments in cases where a dwelling is not habitable and funds for motel or hotel living is clearly warranted. There is nothing in the homeowners policy requiring companies to make advance payments of this kind, but the requirement has been established by the actions of the industry in the past, and would probably be supported by a court of law. The cost of disposing of debris from your property resulting from a loss or disaster is covered under all insurance policies, although such coverage is not written into every policy. The removal is just understood to be a part of any covered loss and therefore part of a valid claim.

As you might imagine, because of the favorable attitude of the courts toward policyholders, insurance companies take extensive measures to protect and reserve their rights under the policy. It is also necessary that company representatives deal fairly with policyholders when adjusting claims. As a result of the attitude of the courts and the vulnerability of insurance companies to bad faith lawsuits, it is uncommon for company personnel to actually cheat policyholders. Claims representatives sometimes appear suspicious simply because the majority of claims are inflated to some degree. In most cases, insurance company personnel will deal with you fairly and will not try to deprive you of payments you deserve.

The Insurance Company Position

Since the adoption of the first statutory fire policy in the late nineteenth century, government agencies and the insurance industry have worked to develop consistency in claims handling. Statutory insurance policies have been adopted by state legislatures outlining minimum allowable coverages and required policy conditions. Numerous standard policies have been introduced and accepted by the insurance industry. Extensive litigation has been instituted as a result of questions regarding interpretation of statutory fire policies and other standard forms, resulting in the accumulation of innumerable legal precedents. Statute law established by legislative groups governs the actions of insurance companies. In spite of the tremendous amount of casebook and statute law which has found its way into the books over the years, there remains considerable room for variation among insurance companies regarding the processing of claims.

The company first must honor its obvious obligations under the policy contract. Then the insurance company is expected to interpret the policy, when necessary, in a manner consistent with case law. However, it is also the responsibility of the company to make decisions on questionable claims where case law and court precedents do not specifically apply. The company also has the prerogative to approach claims in a manner not consistent with court precedents, although such a course of action will carry with it the possibility of adverse legal action.

A basic point to keep in mind is that insurance companies are different, and each has its own unique personality. Company policy on claims handling varies considerably. Most companies bend over backward to find justification for covering losses. If it is possible to find a line of reasoning which enables coverage to be extended to a loss, these companies will provide coverage. The quality of a company's service and attitude toward claims in general is reflected in its approach to questionable claims. In this area appropriate action is not clearly dictated by specific policy language or standard industry practice, and decisions and actions must be left up to individual company policy.

Many companies go to surprising extremes to provide superior service and to satisfy their customers. They do such things as reimburse policyholders for portions of claims which are not covered under the policy. For example, under many homeowners policies, trees are not covered against damage by wind. If a tree blows down onto an insured dwelling, the damage to the house is covered, but the tree itself is not covered. In such a case, the company is obligated only to remove the tree from the dwelling to facilitate repairs. The policy need not respond to the cost of cutting the tree up and hauling away the debris, but some companies extend themselves and not only pay for removal of the tree, but also to have the trunk and larger branches cut up and stacked for the policyholder to be used as firewood!

Most companies are somewhat idiosyncratic in their approach to questionable claims, taking a liberal position in some cases and a conservative one in other cases. The overall attitude of individual companies, however, usually leans in one direction or the other. Approaches to claims are sometimes based on arbitrary company policies that are not in keeping with standard practices and legal rules. At times, incorrect decisions are made by insurance company personnel who do not know any better, and at times unscrupulous practices are followed knowingly.

Questionable Practices

Some companies work tirelessly to minimize payments and to deny as many claims as possible. These companies usually adopt positions on questionable claims which are contrary to the interest of their customers, deciding every question against the policyholder. Some companies go so far as to engage in business practices which are not only unfair, but may be illegal as well. Such companies, fortunately, represent a small minority, but they do exist.

Some practices that these companies engage in to reduce settlements are not correct in a technical sense, but are employed irrespective of technical considerations, legal rules, and industry practices. Some questionable insurance practices are:

- Companies improperly interpret policy language to benefit themselves and use their interpretation as grounds for denying claims or minimizing payments for claims that are actually covered, even though the courts have ruled differently on the policy language.

- Companies reduce settlement amounts on the grounds that there is not enough documentation available to satisfy the company. In these cases a court would probably find the claim in order as submitted.

- Companies sometimes propose compromise settlements (meaning the insured is not paid the full amount of the claim) because of a lack of documentation, violations of policy provisions on the part of an insured, or other factors the company feels may reduce its obligation to the policyholder. At times, a compromise settlement may be appropriate, but such circumstances are rare. Compromise settlements are frequently used by less-than-scrupulous companies as a means of saving money on claims.

- In a situation where a policyholder is unaware that coverage for a portion of a claim exists, a company representative may be inclined to feel that the insured can get along without the payment and neglect to inform the policyholder of the coverage that applies.

The Elements of a Valid Claim

Four criteria must be met in order for a loss to be covered by insurance. Let us look at each criterion in detail.

1. Losses must be accidental—as opposed to events that are certain to occur. A loss caused by an event that is certain to occur would not constitute a valid insurance claim. The reason for the stipulation that losses must be accidental is that insurance policies insure against "risks." If a loss is certain to occur, there is no risk involved. A simple example of a risk might be the chance of one of your windows being broken by a child's baseball. It is not certain to occur, but there is a chance that it will. Let us look at another example to illustrate

a loss that is not accidental, as it is certain to occur. Assume that you contract to have a balcony built onto the second story of your home, with access to it provided by a sliding glass door. Assume that the balcony is slanted several degrees toward the house when completed, and is connected to the house at the same level as the bottom of the door. Further, assume that the bottom of the door is not waterproof.

The first time rainwater falls on your new balcony, it will follow natural laws and flow downhill, beneath the door, and into your house. The resulting loss might not be covered under your insurance policy, as it would be considered the result of a certainty. Recent court decisions that apply to all risk policies have weakened this principle somewhat, although it is still accepted as a valid consideration in some cases.

Losses resulting from deterioration are sometimes thought to be the result of a certainty, as everything wears out eventually. For this reason, most losses caused by deterioration would not be covered by insurance, even if the applicable policy did not specifically exclude deterioration.

2. Losses must be caused by an extraneous factor, meaning an external cause of damage, such as wind damaging your patio furniture. If a loss is not caused by an extraneous factor, and is caused by an inherent physical condition, then the loss would not be covered by insurance.

As an example of an inherent condition, let us return to the case of the new balcony. Suppose that you decide to cover your new balcony with a layer of fiberglass in order to direct the flow of water away from the sliding door. You purchase fiberglass, resin, and hardener from a local hardware store, and mix the hardener into the resin as directed. Two days after completing the job, you notice that the resin has not dried, and is just as wet as it was the day it was applied. You conclude that a crucial ingredient was left out of the hardener at the time it was manufactured, rendering it useless. Your loss then was caused by an inherent condition in a product you purchased—but not by something that happened to the fiberglass, such as an attack by vandals.

3. Losses caused by deliberate actions on the part of a policyholder are not covered.

To return to the example of the new balcony: You sit at your kitchen table, distraught, aggressively gulping your seventh martini. The contractor who built your balcony has disappeared with the wind. The company that manufactured the faulty hardener has been financially drained by class action suits and has declared bankruptcy. (Naturally, it had no product liability insurance.) Half conscious, you get your chain saw out of the garage, and systematically cut sections of the balcony apart, until a scattered pile of clear redwood and sticky fiberglass lies beneath you.

The loss of your balcony would, therefore, not be covered under your insurance policy, as your deliberate actions caused the loss.

4. Covered losses must usually involve legal property. Contraband or illegal items are not covered by insurance, as an insurance contract, like all other contracts, is not valid with respect to illegal property. If you had an illegal whiskey still in your basement, and the still was damaged by a covered peril, coverage for the loss would not exist under your policy. If the still was not being used, however, it might be covered. For example, if the still had belonged to your grandfather and you were merely waiting to sell it for scrap, it might be considered legal property.

While on the subject of the elements of a valid claim, it should be pointed out that in order to have a valid claim, you must actually sustain a loss. It is not enough to have property covered by insurance and to have that property damaged or destroyed by a covered peril.

To illustrate this point, suppose that you have a deteriorated detached garage on your property, which you intend to replace with a new garage. You contract with a wrecking company

to have the garage torn down, and during the first day of
demolition work the roof structure and two walls are removed,
with the remaining walls to be removed the following day. If
the remaining two walls were damaged by fire during the night,
you would not have a loss. The removal of the walls would
be considered a necessary part of the job of replacing the
garage, and the remaining walls would be considered to be
of no value.

There are many and varied circumstances where covered
property is damaged by a covered peril, and a question arises
as to whether or not the policyholder actually suffered a loss.
In such cases, it is the insured's responsibility to demonstrate
that a loss has been sustained when a claim of this kind is
contested by an insurance company.

It is also necessary that a policyholder have a financial and
insurable interest in damaged property in order for a loss to
be sustained. This means that the insured must have some
degree of ownership of or interest in the property, if he is to
have an insurable interest in it. As an example, consider the
case of a homeowner who sells his house. After the sale, the
homeowner might still have an insurance policy on the property
with his name on it. However, if a loss occurred to the property
after the sale, the policyholder would not be entitled to any
payment, as he would not have an insurable interest in the
property at the time of the loss. If a policyholder does not
have an interest in the covered property at the time of a loss,
the policy is considered void with respect to that particular
loss.

Consequential Losses

For the most part, homeowners policies insure against physical
loss, and consequential or remote losses are not covered. A
consequential or remote loss is a loss that is not physical in

nature, but which has been brought about by damage to physical property. If your automatic dishwasher was damaged in a kitchen fire, it would be necessary for you to wash your dishes by hand while you waited for the machine to be repaired. The insurance company would not be liable to you for the cost of renting a dishwasher, nor would they be liable to pay you for the time you spent washing the dishes by hand. The loss of your dishwasher is physical in nature, and the company would be liable to you for the cost of repairing it. The loss of *use* of the dishwasher, however, is not physical in nature and is a consequential loss.

Additional living expense coverages in homeowners policies are intended to compensate policyholders for the consequential loss that results from their home being rendered untenantable by a covered loss, such as a fire. The cost to haul and dump debris consisting of covered property is also a consequential loss, although it is somewhat more physical in nature than the example given above.

Negotiating a Settlement

As a policyholder negotiating the settlement of an insurance claim, you are involved in a business negotiation. It may be hard to be objective, as you will have a personal and emotional view of your situation. To the insurance company, company representatives, and courts that may eventually become involved in your claim, the situation is strictly business, and contract conditions and legal precedents will not be molded to comply with your personal sentiments.

It is easy to lose sight of the unyielding realities of the world of business as a result of your personal involvement in a claim and to neglect to see the forest for the proverbial trees. In order for you to negotiate effectively with company personnel, you must detach yourself from your personal interest in the claim and view things objectively. The fact that you had twenty-seven losses in the past two years that were not reported to the company is not relevant to the processing of a claim you do file. The fact that destroyed property constituting part of your claim had tremendous sentimental value, and is irreplaceable, is not relevant. You may be in a terrible financial position and need money desperately, but do not expect sympathy from insurance companies or courts of law. You are dealing in an area where the rules are established by the printed word and courts' interpretations of those words. Your personal opinions on the issues involved in your claim will have little influence on the people with whom you must reach an agreement.

You will not earn any favors or arouse any sympathy by criticizing the nature of insurance, the insurance company, or by threatening to cancel your policy. You will quickly succeed in making yourself appear foolish if you use fallacious logic in your arguments or insist upon treatment not afforded you under the terms of your policy contract. It is important that you restrict your discussions and negotiations to subjects that are relevant and to subjects that you are familiar with. By being unreasonable in your demands and inaccurate in your perception of the realities of your situation, you will cause company personnel to cease to take you seriously and to deal with you in a condescending manner.

In your dealings with insurance company personnel, consider the position of claims representatives. They are usually people who have "seen all kinds," heard every story, every excuse, every argument, and every complaint. They will typically have a sense of humor, if they have survived the business for any length of time. If you can get the representative to respect your thinking and your arguments, you will be more apt to find the experience of filing a claim agreeable.

You stand your best chance of receiving satisfactory treatment from company personnel when you deal with them in a calm and rational manner. Obviously, you will have a limited knowledge of the subject at hand and an acute lack of experience in the area of claims handling, while the company representative will know all the rules of the game. It is seldom advantageous to arouse the competitive spirit of a claims adjuster by assuming a hostile attitude or by making careless and poorly calculated threats of bad faith lawsuits or reports to the insurance commissioner. Remember, the insurance company wrote the policy. If you put yourself in a position where the representative's expertise and the provisions of the policy are used against you, your struggle may be a long and difficult one.

Negotiation is not necessarily a win-or-lose proposition. It is entirely possible for both parties involved in a negotiation to come out of the negotiation feeling that they have reached a fair and equitable agreement. In negotiating the settlement of an insurance claim, both you and the company representative will have needs to satisfy. You will want to obtain satisfactory compensation for your loss, and the company representative will want to avoid overpaying the claim. It is a common opinion that policyholders want to collect as much money as possible, and that insurance companies want to make the smallest possible payment, but this is not necessarily true.

A claims adjuster will usually feel that a claim has been resolved properly if the claim has been settled within reasonable limits. At times, this means that the adjuster will have to bring down the amount of an inflated claim. This is expected, and is part of the representative's job. In view of this fact, it is appropriate for you to follow one of the foremost rules of negotiation in filing your claim: open the negotiation with an offer that is on the high side. There is no rule that requires the insurance company to accept your proposal blindly, or you to accept theirs. A little horse trading is expected here and is not going to hurt anybody. Assuming a meeting of reasonable minds and a realistic attitude on the part of both parties involved in negotiating settlement of a claim, it should be easy enough to reach a mutually agreeable settlement. If you are slightly aggressive in your approach and do not just sit back and accept a proposal that is not really acceptable to you, you will feel better about the matter, and will benefit financially as well. And the insurance company is not going to give away the store, either. You do not have to worry about the insurance people; they can take care of themselves.

Insurance policies are designed so that policyholders always lose money on an insurance claim, at least in the payment of a deductible. This is as it should be, and the reason is obvious: if it were profitable to file insurance claims, insurance companies would soon go out of business. By the same token, an honest policyholder filing a valid and straightforward claim does not want to lose money on the deal. By being creative in your approach to your claim, and being willing to do a certain amount of work as well, it is entirely possible for you to influence the outcome of the matter so that it is acceptable to you and to the insurance company.

If you find yourself lost in a sea of ignorance and over- whelmed by the baffling world of insurance claims, educate yourself. Get answers to your questions, and research issues unfamiliar to you. This will enable you to deal more effectively in pursuing your claim and might also result in an increase in the number of dollars you receive in payment of your claim. Remember, it is your responsibility to handle your claim prag- matically. The ensuing chapters, it is hoped, will provide help and guidance in this area.

In Sum

When you have to file a claim, keep in mind:

- As a policyholder, you have a strong and favorable position where claims are concerned.
- Courts usually resolve questions on claims in favor of policy- holders.
- The overall effect of court decisions has been to broaden the coverage provided by homeowners policies.

- Insurance companies differ in their approach to claims, and most work to provide their customers with good service.
- Some companies engage in questionable practices, and it is prudent to watch out for activities that might not be proper.
- The elements of a valid claim are:
    1) Losses must be accidental
    2) Losses must be caused by extraneous factors
    3) Losses cannot be caused deliberately by the policy-holder
    4) Covered losses must usually involve legal property
- Consequential losses are not covered by homeowners policies.
- Negotiation is not necessarily a win-lose proposition, and both parties can come out feeling like winners.

⑧ Understanding Replacement Cost Coverage

• The Replacement Cost Provision • Determining Replacement Cost • How the Provision Works • Penalties vs. Actual Cash Value Claims • Replacement Cost Claim Payments • What Constitutes Replacement? • "Betterment" and How It Works

THE term "replacement cost coverage" is a key phrase to understand in insurance considerations. As explained in chapter 4, all of the homeowners policies provide replacement cost coverage to buildings. This coverage is subject to numerous provisions, and it is necessary to fully understand the replacement cost coverage outlined in the policy in order to effectively approach a building claim. The replacement cost provision is important for another reason; without an understanding of the requirements outlined in this portion of the contract, it is impossible to determine how much insurance to buy.

As mentioned earlier, replacement cost coverage applies only to dwellings and other buildings, and not to all property covered under the policy. The policy states that the coverage applies to buildings or building structures, which means structures with a roof and four walls. The term "structure" implies permanence, and an item that is movable, such as a metal storage shed, does not qualify as a building structure. Replacement cost coverage also applies to buildings not connected to the main dwelling, such as pool houses, garages, and the like. Items such as hot tubs, playground equipment, and fences are considered structures, but not buildings, and therefore are not covered for replacement cost. Structures attached to the dwelling, such as decks and patio covers, are considered part of the dwelling, and replacement cost coverage applies.

Certain property, even though part of a building structure, is specifically excluded from replacement cost coverage. This includes radio and television antennas and aerials, carpeting, awnings, domestic appliances, and outdoor equipment, whether they are attached to the building or not. This property is excluded because of its exposure to damage—well illustrated by the case of antennas and awnings—or because it does not have as long a life expectancy as the dwelling itself.

The exclusion of antennas is not very important as antennas are relatively inexpensive items, depreciate slowly, and are not subject to much depreciation. The exclusion of awnings refers to all types of awnings, whether metal, fabric, or wood. This exclusion does not refer to patio covers, which are more substantially built than awnings.

As mentioned, carpeting is excluded from replacement cost coverage. This exclusion refers to carpet that is part of the building. If carpeting is considered a contents item and there is an endorsement attached to the policy that provides replacement cost coverage to contents, then replacement cost coverage would apply to the carpet. A problem sometimes arises with this issue, based on a question about when carpet is a building item and when it is a contents item.

Some companies take the position that carpet installed over a finished floor, such as tile or hardwood, is a contents item. Other companies always consider permanently installed carpet to be part of the building, regardless of the kind of floor over which it is installed. The conflict that comes up is clear: If carpeting is a contents item, and contents are covered for replacement cost, then replacement cost coverage applies—if the carpet is seen as part of the building, then valuation at actual cash value is appropriate.

Any time carpet is installed over an unfinished subfloor, like plywood or concrete, it is undisputedly a building item, and replacement cost coverage will not apply. Even when the carpet is installed over a finished floor, it can be argued that it is a building item. This is because the carpet is permanently attached to the building, and, once installed, would not typically be removed from the premises. The finished floor beneath the carpet would also effectively be destroyed as a result of the carpet installation. Therefore, a company is correct in considering carpet over a finished floor to be a building item and in denying replacement cost coverage to the carpet. Many companies, however, extend the benefit of the doubt to the policyholder in such a situation and provide replacement cost coverage anyway. Because there is a tremendous amount of variation between policies providing replacement cost coverage to personal property, not all of them cover carpeting. Also, some policies contain wording that eliminates this problem. This question is important, because carpeting is vulnerable to damage and is expensive to replace.

As indicated, domestic appliances are also excluded from replacement cost coverage. Some domestic appliances are considered building items. The list includes furnaces, air conditioners, water heaters, fans, built-in refrigerators, stoves, and dishwashers. Any appliance not built in or connected to the building is considered personal property and therefore is not covered for replacement cost, either.

The exclusion from replacement cost of outdoor equipment refers to barbecues, lawnmowers, outdoor furniture, patio and pool equipment, and similar property. This clause specifies that equipment attached to the building and effectively part of it is not covered for replacement cost, for the same reason that this coverage does not apply to domestic appliances.

The Replacement Cost Provision

Statistics show that in approximately 80 percent of all claims cases, less than 10 percent of the property insured is affected by a loss. This means that if a policyholder buys insurance to cover only 10 percent of the property in question, coverage will be adequate 80 percent of the time. At first glance, it might appear advantageous for a policyholder to insure only a small percentage of the property, thus saving money on premiums and assuming the risk of a large loss. However, as insurance companies realize that most losses are small losses, the cost of insuring a small percentage of the property involved would be almost as high as the cost of insuring the property to full value. Furthermore, should the policyholder who insured a small percentage of his property be one of the unlucky few to suffer a large or total loss, it would quickly become evident that the few dollars saved on premiums would have been well spent to purchase insurance on the full value of the property.

In response to the complexity of pricing insurance that would result from insuring property to varying percentages of value, all of the homeowners policies contain a replacement cost provision that requires the policyholder to purchase an amount of insurance equal to 80 percent of the replacement cost of the dwelling. The primary purpose of this requirement is to make the determination of insurance rates simple, allowing premiums to be based on a fixed cost per $100 worth of insurance. If policyholders were to insure their property to varying percentages of value, premiums would have to be based on a sliding scale as the cost of the first $10,000 in coverage would be far greater than the cost of the fourth or fifth $10,000 in coverage.

In view of the pricing structure set up for homeowners policies, as allowed by the 80 percent requirement, if any one policyholder does not insure his house to 80 percent of value, the insurance company is not collecting enough premium for the coverage provided. Where the amount of insurance carried by the policyholder does not comply with the 80 percent requirement, the insurance company will take the position that the policyholder is not entitled to a claim payment based on full replacement cost. The reasoning behind this position is that if the policyholder buys insurance to cover only 50 percent of the required amount, then he is assuming responsibility for the remaining 50 percent. In such a case, if a loss is sustained, the insurance company would pay only 50 percent of the damages. This concept is illustrated in detail later in this chapter.

Determining Replacement Cost

Calculating replacement cost for the purpose of buying insurance is somewhat different than estimating the cost of a new home. The primary difference is that such a calculation need not include the cost of the foundation or the electrical and plumbing fixtures (pipes, conduits, etc.) inside the foundation.

The cost of constructing residential homes is typically calculated on a cost per square foot basis. Naturally, the cost of such construction varies tremendously and is influenced by numerous factors, including the area and type of construction involved. When agents write insurance policies, they calculate replacement cost based on a cost per square foot figure they have experienced to be appropriate for the area and the type of home they are considering.

There are two reasons why it is most important that you accurately determine the replacement cost of your home. First of all, you will want to be certain that your coverage is adequate to comply with the replacement cost requirement. If you rely on your agent's calculations and suggestions and you turn out to be underinsured following a loss, it will be you who will pay the penalty, and not the agent. Second, you will want to be sure that you are not being sold an excessive amount of insurance. If your agent considers a unit cost that is inflated, you will pay premiums on coverage that you do not need and will never be able to use.

If your agent is doing a proper job, the cost data will come from reliable estimating material that is constantly updated. Do not hesitate to ask about the source of your agent's figures. It is also easy enough to obtain such information on your own; libraries and bookstores contain a wide variety of construction cost estimating material that will include the cost of building different types of homes in your area. And most contractors involved in fire restoration work will have concrete ideas about the replacement cost of single family homes. This kind of information can also be obtained from the building inspection and planning departments in your city, as well as from construction cost consultants.

Because construction costs vary, the replacement cost of a dwelling is a relative question. And there are no rules that obligate a policyholder to accept an insurance company's position on the matter. It is a negotiable issue. If a company attempts to attach a penalty to your claim and maintains that you are underinsured, it is your privilege to take exception to the company's position and to submit documentation supporting your contention. Construction cost estimating material can be cited, and replacement cost estimates can be obtained from contractors on a fee basis, if necessary, to support your position.

How the Provision Works

As long as your coverage is sufficient to comply with the 80 percent replacement cost requirement, you will never need to worry about a penalty being applied to a claim. If you sustain a loss, however, and are found to be underinsured, a penalty will be attached to your claim, calculated by a standard formula. The formula is:

$$\frac{\text{Amount of insurance carried}}{\text{Amount of insurance required}} \times (\text{loss} - \text{deductible}) = \text{amount paid}$$

Assume that the replacement cost of your 2,000-square-foot home is estimated to be \$100,000, and that you have it insured for \$65,000. Under the terms of the policy, the amount of insurance required is \$80,000. Further assume that you have a small fire in your kitchen, and the cost to repair is established at \$3,000. If there was no penalty, and a \$100 deductible applied, you would be paid \$2,900. By applying these figures to the above formula, we can calculate the amount of your payment after the penalty. We will consider a \$100 deductible.

$$\frac{\$65,000}{\$80,000} = .8125 \times (\$3,000 - \$100) = \$2,356.25$$

Your payment would be reduced from \$2,900 to \$2,356.25, a difference of \$543.75, providing your claim is paid based on the cost to repair less the appropriate penalty, as opposed to the actual cash value of the cost to repair, which is discussed in the following section.

For obvious reasons, it is important to comply with the replacement cost provision. The formula referred to applies to all losses, large and small. And the greater the extent that you are underinsured, the greater the severity of the penalty.

Penalties vs. Actual Cash Value Claims

When a company is considering attaching a penalty to a claim due to insufficient coverage, the homeowners policies stipulate that payment is to be based on replacement cost less the appropriate penalty *or* the actual cash value of the repairs, whichever is greater. Because of the method used to calculate the actual cash value of repairs and the negotiable nature of this issue, it is frequently best to submit a claim based on the actual cash value of the repairs involved. The following example will illustrate this advice:

Suppose that a distracted and unattentive driver plows his car through your living room wall, leaving a hole the size of a school bus in the side of your house. The cost to repair is $3,000. After measuring your home, the company representative determines that you are severely underinsured. The figures are plugged into the formula outlined, and it is determined that you are 40 percent underinsured, indicating that the amount of your claim is 60 percent of replacement cost. Let us say that your deductible is $100. Therefore, after the application of the penalty, your claim is $1,740.

Assume that the repairs include framing a portion of the affected wall, replacing the interior Sheetrock, stuccoing the exterior, painting the patched wall only on the outside, and repainting the entire living room. We will assume that the flooring or carpet was not damaged.

Clearly, there is no real property improvement involved in the framing, Sheetrock, and stucco repairs. You are simply repairing the damage. The paint on the exterior wall will not match the rest of the house, and so again there would be no improvement to the property. The only repair that might result in a real improvement is the interior paint.

The amount of depreciation to be considered is open to negotiation, and will be based on the condition of the old paint and its age. For the sake of this example, we will consider that the cost of painting the living room is $400 and that the improvement considered is 20 percent of the cost of the repair. This translates to a total reduction of $80 and a claim amount of $2,820 after the deductible. You can see that this is vastly favorable to the $1,740 amount of claim based on replacement cost less the penalty.

Replacement Cost Claim Payments

When claims are paid under the replacement cost coverage in the homeowners policy, the company can figure its obligation three different ways and choose the one that works financially best for the company:

(1) On policy limits—the most the company ever will pay is the amount of insurance that applies to the property covered, be it a dwelling or an appurtenant structure.

(2) On the cost of replacement—based on the cost of an equivalent building at the same location.

(3) On the actual amount spent in completing repairs.

In the case of losses over $1,000, the policyholder must complete repairs in order to collect the full amount of replacement cost. For its part, the insurance company is required to pay the amount of the actual cash value of the repairs. The difference between the actual cash value amount and the full replacement cost is paid after the policyholder shows that the work has been done and substantiates the cost of the work.

Remember that the company only owes the amount of the money spent, even if the estimate used to conclude the claim was higher than the actual cost of the job. Let us look at an example to illustrate this concept. Assume that you have a small fire in your garage, resulting in damage to the structure estimated at $4,000. The company might pay $3,000 upon completion of adjustment of the claim, considering this amount to be the actual cash value of repairs, leaving an outstanding replacement cost claim of $1,000. The company, therefore, would be obligated to pay you the remaining $1,000 after the repairs were completed and after you demonstrated that the work actually cost $4,000. If your neighbor happened to wander over and tell you that he could do the work for $3,500 and you had him do it for that price, the company would only owe you an additional $500.

The policyholder also has another obligation in the matter of replacement cost claims: He must take some form of action on a replacement cost claim within 180 days from the date of loss. The clauses that include this stipulation vary among policies, and there are two schools of thought on interpretation of the clauses. One interpretation is that the policyholder must notify the company of an intention to make claim under the replacement cost coverage within 180 days, but it is not necessary that the claim be prepared and submitted within that time. In spite of the fact that a company may set a deadline for filing a replacement cost claim based on a reasonable time for the completion of repairs, it is felt that the company does not have firm grounds for requiring that the claim actually be submitted by a certain date. The other school of thought is that the company can require submission of the claim within the 180-day period. The position of a company on this question will depend on the policy involved and on the company's interpretation of that policy. If this becomes a question on a claim, the prudent thing to do is to write the company, and find out what its position is.

Under the replacement cost coverage, the insurance company is obligated to pay full replacement cost on all losses under $1,000 as soon as the claim is adjusted, whether repairs are completed or not. The company furthermore cannot require a policyholder to show how much was actually spent in completing repairs. For practical reasons, many companies pay full replacement cost initially on claims far larger than $1,000 as a matter of policy, without requiring submission of a replacement cost claim by the policyholder. By doing so, the company can handle claims more efficiently and expeditiously, as the cost of keeping files open until repairs are completed and making two separate payments on relatively small claims is expensive and consumes manpower time. In negotiating a claim on a dwelling or structure, it is sometimes beneficial to ask that the replacement cost payment be made at the outset, although it is important to recognize that the company has the right to require that the claim be handled in keeping with the terms of the policy.

What Constitutes Replacement?

Replacement cost can be defined as the cost to replace damaged property with like kind and quality, similar in basic style, quality, and function. It is important to recognize that the policy provides coverage for *replacement* cost and not *reproduction* cost. Reproduction cost is the cost of replacing property exactly as it was, down to the last detail. The 1971 policy uses the word "identical" in outlining the company's liability, and some people in the industry interpret this to mean that the policy should respond to reproduction costs. This is a position that will be met with resistance by most claims representatives. We will use an example to clarify the difference between replacement cost and reproduction cost and the potential increase in cost that reproduction cost can entail. Imagine that an elaborate balustrade with a detailed handrail and lathe-turned balusters was destroyed by fire. In all probability, it would be possible to buy prefabricated materials, including the handrail and balusters that closely resembled the damaged items, for a reasonable price. If the insurance company were to pick up the tab to make identical items, the cost would double or triple because the parts of the balustrade would have to be custom-made, which would involve expensive milling work.

In order to establish its limit of liability under the replacement cost coverage, the insurance company is required only to consider the cost of building an identical structure at the same location. Alterations necessitated by building code requirements are not to be included. It goes without saying that the company is not required to pay for any work that upgrades the property; only similar kind and quality will be considered. Covered repairs will be limited to the work necessary to return the property to the condition it was in prior to the loss.

There is one interesting loophole in replacement cost coverage: the repair work done to the building need not be based on replacing identical property at the same location. In some states, reconstructing property at any location, including a different city or state, will qualify a replacement cost claim. Furthermore, the policyholder is entitled to the full replacement cost, no matter how or where the property is replaced, as long as the money is spent for replacement of property.

Some companies question alterations made while reconstructing a dwelling that are applied to a replacement cost claim. They take the position that any variation in reconstruction that can be considered an improvement is not a valid portion of a replacement cost claim. As an example, if you have to settle a claim based on the cost of replacing pine cabinets in your kitchen, and were to get oak units installed for the same price, certain companies might resist paying the entire cost of the cabinets. Other companies feel that it is not the company's position to consider the kind of work involved, and that the policy is obligated to respond to the full replacement cost of reconstruction as long as the money is spent repairing the building.

The question, "What constitutes replacement?" is also relevant to replacement cost policies on personal property. Should a policyholder be required to replace the affected property with identical items, such as a stereo set with a similar stereo set, or does the purchase of any form of personal property satisfy the requirement that the property is replaced? The policy language in the various policies and endorsements sometimes speaks to this question, although there is considerable room for differing interpretations of the wording in many cases.

It can well be argued that insurance companies are not in a position to stipulate how replacement cost payments are dispersed in this respect, once they have agreed on a given cost to repair. A replacement cost insurance policy provides a certain degree of compensation for a loss. If one form of real or personal property is replaced with another form of real or personal property of equal value, the degree of compensation remains the same.

"Betterment" and How It Works

As you well know by now, the field of insurance contains many terms, and another important one is the word "betterment." Betterment refers to the increase in value to a piece of property resulting from improvements to it. If a house damaged by fire is completely renovated and effectively remodeled in the process, the end product is a newer, better, and more valuable house than the old one. The term "depreciation," by contrast, refers to the concept that an item becomes less valuable as it wears out or is used up. The terms betterment and depreciation are frequently used synonymously in the insurance industry, and have a similar effect on the processing of insurance claims.

In a technical sense, the degree of betterment or improvement to real property after renovation can only be measured by the actual increase in value that results from the renovation. This means that it may be impossible on a practical level to calculate the actual amount of betterment involved following the repair of a building. In order to do so, it would be necessary to determine the amount the property would have brought on the open market immediately prior to the loss and the amount the property would sell for following repairs. The resulting difference would be the amount of real betterment or improvement.

Obviously, it is rarely possible to obtain accurate betterment figures for the purpose of adjusting an insurance claim. Therefore, insurance companies do what they consider to be the next best thing. They estimate the amount of betterment resulting from the repairs. This is done either by considering an amount of betterment based on a percentage of the overall cost to repair—meaning the total cost of the job—or based on a percentage of the cost of individual repairs.

There is no rule that precludes the company from calculating betterment on the total cost of the job. It is commonly felt that it is improper to do so. Such a practice considers betterment on each part of the repair work, which may not be correct in view of the real definition of betterment. There are certain repairs that do not constitute betterment in any real sense, although they involve replacing old property with new. A good example of this would be new studs in a wall; they are not any more valuable than the old ones. Conversely, new and more stylish vinyl flooring in a kitchen might realistically increase the value of the house, perhaps to an extent greater than the cost of the new floor.

When calculating betterment on individual repairs, it is improper for a company to depreciate all repairs, as some will not improve the property in any way. Only repairs that represent improvements should be depreciated. It is necessary to look at the actual degree of improvement (and added value in terms of dollars) that results from the repair in question. If new interior paint is included in a claim, for example, the amount of depreciation should be based on the age and condition of the old paint. Such an approach to the question of betterment on buildings might be met with resistance by some adjusters, but it is a theoretically sound position and a valid argument in negotiating the amount of betterment applied to a building claim.

When calculating betterment on building repairs for practical purposes, the criteria used should be replacement cost less depreciation and the ratio between the life expectancy and the age of the item. Different betterment figures will apply to various repairs, based on the expected life of the part of the building involved. In many cases, the condition of the building will speak for itself. If plaster is crumbling from the lath, appreciable betterment might be in order. By contrast, if new ceramic tile will not look any better than the old tile, then only a minor amount of betterment would be appropriate.

A well-built structure will stand for 50 to 75 years without major renovation, and will depreciate at roughly 1½ to 2 percent per year. This holds true for the structural portions of a building, including framing, subfloors, doors, windows, siding, stucco, plaster, plumbing pipes, Sheetrock, insulation, cabinetry, and the like. Other parts of a dwelling will depreciate at different rates, depending upon the degree of wear and tear. The following table provides a general rate of depreciation per year for various parts of a structure:

Part of Structure	Rate of Depreciation
Shake roofs	4 to 5%
Composition roofs	5%
Exterior paint	15 to 20%
Interior paint	10 to 20%
Sheet vinyl flooring	5 to 10%
Floor tile	4 to 7%
Hardwood floor finish	4 to 10%
Carpet	10 to 20%
Electrical wiring	4%
Water heaters	4 to 7%
Heaters and air conditioners	3 to 5%

To better understand the concept of betterment and its practical application, let us consider an example: Imagine that a fire in your kitchen damages the cabinets, Formica counter top, and paint, and that the vinyl flooring is ruined by water used to put out the fire.

We will assume that the cost to repair is established, to the company's satisfaction, at $2,400. When broken down into categories, the repair prices are:

Cabinet repairs	$ 400
Formica	800
Flooring	800
Paint	400
Total	$2,400

If the company representative wanted to calculate betterment on the overall cost to repair, he might propose an allowance for betterment of 35 percent, which would translate into $840. This would indicate an actual cash value of repairs of $1,560. If betterment was based on the cost of the individual repairs, the numbers would likely be different. There would be no real improvement to the cabinets, as they would be repaired and not replaced. For the sake of our example, we will assume that the Formica was a contemporary style, and that the flooring and paint were in relatively poor condition. This means that betterment of 10 percent might apply to the Formica, and 40 percent might apply to the flooring and paint. Total betterment, then, would be $560. It is evident that this is more favorable than the total betterment based upon the overall cost of repairs. Keep in mind that if the company wanted to make payment on an actual cash value basis initially, you would have to complete the work and prove that $2,400 was spent in doing so in order to collect the amount of the betterment. This might be slightly difficult if you made changes in the repairs that were considered improvements by the company.

Understanding replacement cost coverage is vital to the compiling and handling of claims, a subject that is dealt with in the next two chapters.

In Sum

When studying replacement cost coverage, keep in mind:

- Replacement cost coverage applies only to buildings, and not to all property covered under the policy.
- You should be aware of the kinds of property that are excluded from replacement cost coverage.
- The replacement cost provision is one of the most important parts of a homeowners policy, and should be thoroughly understood by the policyholder.
- You must take an active role in determining the replacement cost of your home. This task should not be left to your agent or the company.
- Be aware of how the replacement cost provision works, and how penalties are attached to claims.
- A claim payment based on actual cash value is usually better than a claim payment based on a penalty, when the property involved is not adequately insured.
- There are various alternatives for the payment of replacement cost claims, and you should try and negotiate the method of payment that works best for you.
- The question "what constitutes replacement?" can be critical in filing a replacement cost claim.
- An understanding of the concept of "betterment" is important to the process of filing a claim, and can be used to your benefit.

9 Steps to Compiling Claims on Dwellings

• Four Steps to Compiling a Claim • Variations on Reconstruction • Overhead and Profit • Building Code Requirements • Dealing with Contractors • Reviewing the Estimate • Payment Assignments • Penalty Clauses

COMPILING a claim for damaged dwellings or other structures is an involved and complicated process. There are numerous decisions to be made in the early stages and along the way that will greatly influence the end result. If the questions involved are approached systematically and are properly addressed throughout the process, the outcome will be as beneficial as possible.

Four Steps to Compiling a Claim

The four steps to compiling a claim are:

1) Determining coverages
2) Determining the scope of repairs

117

3) Determining the cost to repair
4) Determining the amount of the claim

Step 1—Determining Coverages

It is critical to determine almost immediately what is covered by your policy and what is not. The reason is simple—differences between the cost to repair and the amount of claim will mean out-of-pocket expenses to the policyholder. If coverage is lacking in certain areas, it will be necessary to take measures throughout the adjustment process to cover the shortage by arranging to have some money left over to pay for items that are not covered.

In the best of all possible circumstances, everything will be covered for full replacement cost, and the policyholder will pay only the policy deductible. In the majority of cases, however, that will not be the circumstances. There will be several gaps in coverage. The most obvious problem areas involve property not covered for replacement cost, as mentioned in chapter 8. This property, as you know, includes carpeting, appliances, awnings, and outdoor equipment. It will be depreciated. You may also have landscaping (tree and shrub) damage, and the cost to repair may exceed the policy limit that applies to such property. In any event, the probability is high that there will be parts of any claim that are not fully covered, and the resulting deficit may be hundreds or thousands of dollars.

Early in the adjustment process, most claims representatives do not identify the parts of a loss that are not covered and the areas where betterment applies. Such issues are frequently raised after all of the figures are established and settlement is pending. At the time of the representative's first inspection of the property, it should be requested that all problem areas be identified. This is also the time to address questions of coverage. Read the policy, talk to your agent or an insurance attorney, and satisfy yourself that the adjuster's interpretation of the policy is correct.

Step 2—Determining the Scope of Repairs

The "scope of repairs" is the insurance company's description of work to be included in repair estimates. It is sometimes referred to as a "scope of damage," a "description of work," or a "job description," and is also seen in the form of a fully itemized repair estimate. In most cases, a scope of repairs will be prepared by the claims representative. Some adjusters leave the task of determining the work to be included in repair bids to a contractor. In such a case, the contractor will review the damages—frequently in the company of the adjuster—and then will prepare an estimate that will be used to conclude the adjustment. The policyholder may not be consulted about the contractor or informed of the work included until settlement is proposed. Furthermore, it may be assumed between the representative and the contractor that the policyholder will allow the contractor to complete the repair work.

As a policyholder, you should clearly inform the claims representative that you have an interest in the scope of repairs, and that you wish to go over the work to be considered in the estimates before they are prepared. Be sure to be present at the time the representative makes the inspection of the premises, and go over the damages in detail, item by item and room by room. Be certain that all necessary work is included; it might be a good idea to make a list of your own, itemized room by room. Since the cost to repair will be based upon the scope of work, you will want to be certain that all work you deem necessary is included. A higher cost to repair will mean more money to work with in the end, and a thorough approach to determining the scope of repairs will increase the probability that sufficient funds will be available to complete repairs.

Certain aspects of a scope of repairs are clear-cut. It will be obvious, for instance, that when an entire roof structure is destroyed, it must be replaced. In some cases, the scope of repairs will be determined in part by city building inspectors.

A homeowners policy does not pay for city code requirements unless an inspector stipulates that a section of framing or other part of a building be replaced because the damage could weaken the structure. Then it can be included in the scope of repairs.

There are usually some questionable aspects of a scope of repairs. A company representative, for example, may feel that a back bedroom was not damaged sufficiently by smoke to warrant painting it. Or he may feel that soiled carpets should be cleaned rather than replaced. It may be that a parquet floor scratched by fire-fighting activities may not be included. Cabinetry damaged by smoke may be cleaned and refinished, and not replaced. In the long run, simple common sense will adequately dictate if the work in question is actually necessary and should be included in the scope of repairs.

Adjusters sometimes attempt to get a policyholder to accept alterations that result in a lower cost to repair. It might be suggested that plaster be replaced with Sheetrock. Such an alteration might be acceptable if there is a benefit provided in exchange, such as the company agreeing to pay full replacement cost on carpeting. However, any such deviations from "like kind and quality" in the scope of repairs will result in a lower cost to repair and a lower overall settlement. You have the right to insist that the scope of repairs include all work necessary to return the structure to the condition it was in before the loss; it is the prudent thing to do in most cases.

Step 3—Determining the Cost to Repair

At this point in the adjustment, you have agreed with the company representative on the scope of repairs and will have a detailed itemization of the work to be included in the estimates. The next step is to convert the scope of repairs into an agreed cost to repair, a process which is critical to the outcome of the adjustment; it can also be a volatile issue. For this reason, it is important to keep your relationship with the representative amicable. For as a policyholder, your position here is a weak one.

There are two primary reasons for this. The first is that it is proper and usual for a company to use an estimate it obtains to establish the cost to repair. This means that a company representative can obtain a bid from a familiar contractor and conclude the adjustment on the amount of the estimate. And betterment can be considered against the amount of the estimate as well. The second reason is that the company in its contract *always* retains the right to repair the property. Insurance companies do not typically desire to use this contract option because in doing so they can become liable for the actions of the contractor or can be considered to warrant the contractor's work. If this option is used by the company, your chances of handling the claim creatively in order to avoid absorbing any shortfalls are ruined.

In most cases, the claims representative will take an active role in determining the cost to repair. Representatives' methods of operation in this respect vary considerably from company to company. Many representatives obtain one estimate from a familiar contractor, leaving the policyholder to secure a competitive bid. A good many representatives try to leave policyholders out of the process altogether for the simple reason that a contractor familiar to the representative will come in with a price that is not a surprise, and because the estimate is usually open to negotiation if the figures are not acceptable. In rare instances, the representative may request that the policyholder obtain estimates, concluding the claim based on the low bid if the price is agreeable. This kind of situation is most advantageous to the policyholder; it is, however, uncommon.

Irrespective of the position of the company representative, you will want to obtain one or two estimates on your own for your use. If the company representative fully intends to conclude the claim on the basis of estimates obtained from familiar contractors, it is really useless for you to submit any estimates to the insurance company. The estimates you obtain, however, can be used by you in your own personal involvement in having the dwelling or structure repaired. Your estimates should be from one or two contractors that you would be willing to have do the work, and that you think will give you a favorable price. These estimates will tell you what the work will actually cost you. If the insurance company requests that you submit estimates, they should be higher than the others. Otherwise the claim payment will not cover the cost of the work you want done.

You will be more likely to obtain high estimates from certain kinds of contracting companies than from others. Union firms usually charge more than nonunion companies, so you might want to look for a union shop. It is also typical for large firms to charge more than small firms, so you should check the size of the company you are dealing with. Firm size can be roughly determined by the extent of the office facility, the number of trucks sitting around, etc. A firm's reputation for extremely high quality work also is an indication of that firm's prices. (Remember, top-quality work usually brings top-dollar prices!) If you find a large union company with a good reputation, you can expect to get an estimate that will be at the upper end of the spectrum. If you need assistance locating contractors who will bid your job or who are experienced in insurance work, your broker or agent may be able to refer you to such firms in your area.

In determining the lowest cost of the work you want done, you will need to seek out smaller, possibly nonunion companies. Obviously, it is beneficial to check on the reputation of the companies you are considering; ask to see some of their work. At this point, you should take into account any alterations you might be considering when the repairs are made. Estimates submitted to the insurance company, however, should always be based on the scope of the work. The bids obtained for your own use may include the alterations under consideration.

After you have obtained your own estimates, you will have

an idea of the cost of the work you want to do, including your alteration plans, and if the company has asked you to submit a bid, you will also have an estimate that is higher than the actual cost of repairs. You will then be in a position to negotiate the cost to repair with the company.

In all likelihood, the adjuster will have an estimate as well. If the representative desires to conclude the adjustment on the basis of a bid obtained by the company, there is little you can do about it. It is possible, however, to compare your estimate against the representative's bid and to discuss differences between the two. Check to see if the representative's bid clearly includes all of the work included in the scope of damage. If something has been left out, an allowance should be added for the item. If the estimate is not sufficiently detailed, you may be able to request that the representative confirm what work is to be included in the estimate and to obtain a detailed description of work from the contractor who prepared the estimate. Inquire about the quality of the work to be performed; this may also be an area of discussion.

An insurance company needs a licensed contractor's estimate to stand firm on a repair cost figure. If for some reason the company's contractor will not honor the estimate, the company has to obtain another one or conclude the claim on the basis of an estimate you submit.

In negotiating the final cost to repair, your goal is to obtain a payment sufficient to have all of the necessary work done. Once the company has made a commitment to consider a given cost to repair, you can turn your attention to negotiating the final amount of the claim and to deciding how the money will be spent in repairing the building.

Step 4—Determining the Amount of Claim

Once the cost to repair is established, determining the amount of claim is relatively easy. All of the appropriate deductions are simply subtracted from the cost to repair. The deductible will always apply, and must be considered. Betterment will also apply to the items excluded from replacement cost coverage, but must be negotiated. Parts of the loss that are not covered at all may be subtracted from the cost to repair. For example, work necessary to comply with a building code regulation may be mistakenly included in an estimate; it, of course, is not covered. When all of the deductions are considered, the result is the amount of claim at replacement cost.

If payment is to be made on an actual cash value basis initially, with the balance payable subsequent to completion of repairs and submission of a replacement cost claim, the actual cash value claim will be calculated. This is another amount that must be negotiated and may be important if a replacement cost claim will be difficult to collect. In some cases, if the actual cash value claim amount is high enough and your own cost to repair is low enough, it may be advantageous to waive the right to make claim under the replacement cost coverage. This will eliminate the possibility of disputes arising over resulting improvements of the property. For example, if you were to be paid the actual cash value amount for some wallpaper, and then installed paneling instead of wallpaper, the company might hesitate to pay the full replacement cost claim, arguing that the paneling was an improvement. If the actual cash value payment on the wallpaper was enough to pay fully for the paneling, you would not have to worry about collecting the amount of the replacement cost claim.

Once all of the figures are agreed upon, including the cost to repair, the actual cash value amount of claim, and the pending replacement cost claim, you will sign the papers, collect the actual cash value payment in full, and turn your attention to repairing the damage.

Variations on Reconstruction

Once your claim has been paid, there are two ways to approach doing the repair work so that the situation works to your greater benefit. One way is to find a contractor willing to do the work for less money than the cost to repair used to conclude the claim. The other way is to change the reconstruction work on the dwelling so that a cost savings results.

There are many possible variations in reconstructing dwellings, and any alteration that results in a savings is worth considering. In older houses, there is usually a greater opportunity to cut construction costs than in newer homes. For instance, plaster can be replaced with Sheetrock, wood windows with aluminum, hardwood floors with carpet, leaded glass with standard panes, etc. In fact, it may be necessary to consider such alterations in repairing older buildings as there is likely to be a greater number of code violations to be addressed, and the money saved can be used to cover the cost of the code work. By contrast, there may be little room to cut corners in newer structures. They usually have Sheetrock walls, simple trim, basic cabinetry, aluminum windows, plywood or concrete subfloors covered with carpet, all of which are inexpensive to replace.

Some possible variations on reconstruction include:

- Plaster can be replaced with Sheetrock—savings to 100 percent.
- Wood sash and double-hung windows can be replaced with aluminum—savings to 50 percent.
- Panel doors can be replaced with standard prehung doors—savings from 10 to 300 percent.
- Milled trim, molding, etc. can be replaced with available standard moldings that will eliminate the expense of manufacturing and milling custom doors, window trim, base moldings, etc.—savings to 400 percent.
- Wood balustrades with milled rails and banisters can be re-

placed with solid Sheetrock balustrades with a prefabricated rail—savings of 200 percent.

- Wood paneling, plate moldings, wainscoting, etc. can be omitted altogether. Savings are considerable, as custom woodwork in hardwood is extremely expensive.
- Marble and terrazzo entryways or foyers can be replaced with ceramic tile or brick—savings to 500 percent.
- Fireplace mantles and facings can be altered or omitted altogether.
- Hutch-type cabinets, sometimes fitted with leaded glass, can be constructed simply or omitted altogether.
- Wallpaper can be substituted for wood paneling, or both can be omitted altogether.
- Hardwood floors can be replaced with plywood subflooring and wall-to-wall carpet—savings to 300 percent.
- Ceramic tile can be replaced with vinyl tile on floors or Formica on counter tops—savings to 300 percent.
- Hardwood and/or custom cabinets can be replaced with prefab units—savings to 300 percent.
- Sprayed acoustic ceilings can be painted instead of resprayed, or omitted altogether.
- Shake roofing can be replaced with composition shingles—savings to 150 percent.

The foregoing represents only a partial list of potential alterations. There are certainly greater possibilities available when replacing appliances, lighting and plumbing fixtures, and the like. Sometimes it may be advantageous to consider even greater alterations in construction and design. Floor plans can be altered, rooms can be added or changed, etc.

When considering alternative methods of construction, it is important to understand the effect such alterations will have on the value of the building. Alterations frequently involve a trade-off in terms of value. If a marble entryway is tiled, a reduction in value will result unless the tile is far more stylish and attractive than the marble. The same holds true with many of the possible substitutions mentioned. An alternative design or method of construction, however, does not always mean a reduction in value—if executed properly, it can mean just the opposite. If dated lighting fixtures in a kitchen and bathrooms are replaced with more modern, stylish designs, an increase in value may result. Property owners have long known that remodeling frequently carries with it the reality of improvement and appreciation. So in exploring alteration ideas, keep in mind the opportunity available to modernize and revitalize. In some cases, it is advantageous to reconstruct in keeping with the flavor of the original structure, but do not overlook possibilities that will allow you to have both cost savings and appreciation too.

Some of the alternative repairs available will have advantages that go beyond a cost savings. Granted, Sheetrock does not have the soundproofing or fire rating qualities plaster has, but it is more resistant to damage by water and to cracking due to stress or earth movement. It is also easier to install and to patch. A house with interior Sheetrock is almost as valuable as a plaster house, given equal design and quality of finish. Composition roofing is much less expensive than shake roofing, and has the advantage of being much more fire resistant. Aluminum windows are another alternative repair with advantages. They cost far less than old-fashioned wood sash windows, and they do not deteriorate as rapidly with age. They also seal more tightly, require virtually no maintenance whatsoever, and can be attractive to boot.

Before considering any possible variations on reconstruction, it is important to determine the insurance company's position with respect to alterations included in replacement cost claims. The question raised in the previous chapter, "What constitutes replacement?" is highly relevant here. As pointed out, some companies feel it is none of their business to police the repairing or reconstructing of the insured building, and will pay up to the agreed cost to repair as long as the money is spent repairing the structure. Other companies are hesitant to pay for repairs that might be considered improvements, regardless of the cost of such repairs. Some companies actually pay their personnel to inspect damaged property after repairs have been completed in order to confirm that the repairs are consistent with the original design of the house. It is, therefore, essential that you establish the company's position on this question before you complete alternative repairs. Be sure to get a response in writing. A simple letter from the company confirming the company's position will suffice. If you do not get a letter, you may run into resistance when filing your replacement cost claim. If you do get resistance, it may be a good idea to seek the advice and assistance of an insurance attorney.

Some adjusters feel that any alteration in reconstruction involves a trade-off in value since if a given amount of money is spent on construction, the value of the property is increased by exactly that amount of money, regardless of how it is spent. In the case of a kitchen remodeling, for example, one could install expensive flooring and inexpensive cabinets, or vice versa, and assume that the overall value of the work was the same either way, given equal quality of design. Admittedly, this might not be wholly true in practice—a floor installed by a nonunion worker will have the same value as one installed by a union tradesman, given equal quality of work, although the nonunion price may be much lower—but represents a strong theoretical argument that an insurance company has no right to dictate the kind of work included in a replacement cost claim.

Overhead and Profit

Overhead and profit allowances are included in construction estimates by contractors to cover their operating costs and to provide profit. Some insurance companies maintain that a policyholder is not entitled to be paid the overhead and profit amount included in an estimate unless a contractor is actually involved in every aspect of the repair work. This issue usually comes up when alternative repairs are made by policyholders and included as part of a replacement cost claim, or when cash payments for claims are made to policyholders. In a practical sense, this means that if you wanted to have a contractor do the heavy construction work on a job and do the painting yourself, the company might refuse to pay you the profit and overhead amount on the cost of the painting.

The rationale for this position is that the policyholder is not a contractor, does not have the contractor's overhead expenses, and, most importantly, is not entitled to profit from a loss. The homeowners policies do not specifically address this issue and do not state that a policyholder is precluded from profiting from a loss. For this reason, many adjusters feel that a policyholder is entitled to payment based on the full cost of repairs and that it is his option to pay a contractor the overhead and profit allowance or to keep it. If a policyholder is acting as his own contractor, payment for such work is appropriate. A homeowner acting as a contractor has many of the expenses of a real contractor—paint brushes, thinner, dropcloths, time involved in picking up materials, time spent phoning subcontractors, etc. If an insurance company agrees to a certain cost to repair, it should be obligated to consider the full cost to get the work done and to make payment accordingly. This is another negotiable issue and an area where an insurance company's position is open to question.

Overhead and profit allowances are an appropriate and necessary part of a repair estimate. The amount of overhead and profit included varies, and is usually between 10 percent and 30 percent. The expenses and allowances included in this category are sometimes broken down in different ways or labeled differently, and called builders fees, etc. Regardless of the method of itemization and labels used, everything over and above the job cost (the total of all labor, material, and subcontract prices) goes to the general contractor to cover his overhead and to provide profit.

Building Code Requirements

In any reconstruction project, building code requirements are a concern, although they may not necessarily be a problem. Building inspectors will be assigned to review and pass the work at various stages of completion and to comment on the acceptability of the types of repairs considered. Whether the code work necessary involves five hundred or five thousand dollars, it is a hurdle that must be surmounted if the house is to be habitable.

The job of the building inspector is to ensure that repaired buildings are safe and habitable, and that they comply with existing code requirements. Code requirements vary tremendously from city to city. Every contractor knows the personalities of building inspectors vary as well, making any given job a breeze or a nightmare, depending upon the inspector assigned to the job. The building inspector is a civil servant and has the full authority of a large bureaucracy as a support system. It is obvious, then, that it is much more beneficial to work with the inspector than to take an adversarial position.

Before construction work begins, discuss the code work necessary with your contractor. If he is experienced in insurance work, he will have a good idea of the problems involved. He may also be able to offer some suggestions for alternative repairs which will circumvent problems. A creative approach to code work is also effective after building inspectors are involved. Most inspectors know that rebuilding a structure after a fire or other loss is difficult and complicated, and most are flexible in their demands. Inspectors are frequently willing to draw on their experience and offer suggestions and assistance in solving any problems that arise.

It is sometimes difficult to foresee all of the potential code problems that may surface in the course of construction. There is no surefire way to avoid surprises, and one can only prepare as well as possible. There are numerous areas where code requirements may present problems. Some are:

- An inspector may require that concrete piers or a concrete foundation be installed in the case of older post-and-beam structures, where the structural members are resting on bare soil or where a basement floor is dirt.
- A building inspector may require that portions of the structure affected by wet or dry rot be replaced at the time repairs are made.
- Alterations in the superstructure may be required. Additional members may be called for, or more substantial material may be stipulated. Modern codes may call for roof rafters sixteen inches on center and two-by-four-inch studs, where an older building may have been built with the rafters twenty-four inches apart and two-by-three-inch studs. Such requirements do not usually mean a substantial increase in cost, as the cost of the additional rough framing material is nominal and the cost of labor increases very little.
- Unsafe materials, including those controlled by the Occupational Safety and Health Administration (OSHA), may be discovered, and the cost to remove and replace them may well go beyond the scope of repairs prepared by the adjuster. Other nonapproved materials may be found, such as particle board used in place of plywood, or beaverboard used in place of Sheetrock, and replacement may be called for.
- Electrical code requirements are one of the most common sources of additional expenses. When a substantial portion of the electrical wiring in a house is damaged, code laws frequently call for complete rewiring of the dwelling and compliance of the entire system with modern codes. This can

mean replacing all of the switches, receptacles, and fixtures in the house, and all of the wiring, as well as replacing the main panel and breaker box. Bringing electrical systems up to code requirements in an older home can also involve the addition of numerous outlets and fixtures, not all of which will be included in the insurance claim.

- Heating systems may also be cited for alteration by a building inspector. A wall furnace is sometimes required in place of a floor furnace or freestanding heater. Water heaters may have to be elevated, vented differently, or changed altogether. Flue pipes and vents may require alteration, as modern codes call for double wall flues in some cases; common flues may also be split, with a separate vent noted for each appliance.

- Building inspectors also indicate alterations in the case of property that is poorly maintained or deteriorated. Cracked and peeling flooring, loose ceramic tiles, cracked shower doors or enclosures, worn wood sash windows, ill-fitting doors, and the like may draw the attention of an inspector and may be earmarked for replacement. Part of the inspector's job is to see to it that the repaired structure is sound; thus, an interest in the overall structural integrity of the building is appropriate.

- In most municipalities, code laws give the buildings department the right to require that an entire building be demolished and rebuilt when a portion of it is damaged. For example, the requirement might give the city the right to require such work if 40 or 50 percent of a structure is damaged. Obviously, this represents a serious threat to a homeowner. In practical terms, however, it is rare that complete demolition of a building is required when it is possible to repair the building. Building inspectors know that such a requirement is a devastating blow to the building owner, and most buildings departments need a good reason to require demolition of a partially damaged building. Usually, the building must be unsafe to begin with, or must be loaded with code violations before this kind of code law is drawn upon by a building inspector. The homeowners policies, incidentally, do not insure against this kind of situation, although insurance can be purchased to cover this risk.

The foregoing list of examples is far from complete. Plumbing, roofing, illegal additions or fixtures (patio covers, storage sheds, etc.), and general floor plan layout are all areas of interest to the observant building inspector and present potential problems. Sometimes repair to a small part of a structure will necessitate code work to a much larger portion. The key to dealing with code problems is to do everything possible to anticipate the problems, find the most creative ways of solving them, work to cover the cost of the alterations in the amount paid on the claim, and hope for the best.

Dealing with Contractors

The relationship between contractors and insurance companies is sometimes closely intertwined and can appear paradoxical. In view of the close working relationship between the two and the deep involvement of the contractor in the adjustment process, it may look as if the contractor is working for, or at least in conjunction with, the insurance company representative. Contractors may even make direct statements indicating that the company representative has "given" them a job, or that they work "for" a specific company. The simple fact of the matter is this: The insurance company, as mentioned, has the right to repair or replace the damaged property. If it chooses to exercise that right, it is responsible for hiring the contractor, which includes signing the contract and all the responsibility that goes along with it. If the company does not choose to repair or replace, it has absolutely no say in the repair process; the way the money is spent is between the policyholder and the mortgage company, if there is one.

It is typical for a contractor to present the policyholder with a contract to be signed after the claim has been concluded by the company based upon the contractor's bid. There may be tremendous deficiencies in the payment as a result of depreciated items, gaps in coverage, code alterations, etc. The policyholder may not be notified of these problems until after final settlement of the claim, when the construction contract is signed. This is advantageous to the insurance company for several reasons. The company can settle a claim quickly this way, and can be sure that only the appropriate items are included in the estimate. It also has a valid estimate to use as a solid basis for settlement of the claim. It is also advantageous to the contracting firm, which gets the work. Obviously, it is not always the best deal in the world for the policyholder. In such a situation, the policyholder has the right to refuse to hire the contractor or to sign the construction contract.

As stated, most insurance companies do not like to exercise their option to repair or replace, because they sometimes become liable for the contractor's actions and may sometimes be seen to warrant the contractor's work. Even if the company's involvement is limited to calling the contractor and referring the contracting firm to the policyholder, it might be seen to warrant the construction work. As insurance companies do not typically want to become active in the construction business, they tend to avoid signing construction contracts. They simply do not want the liability exposure. They usually prefer to remain legally detached from the agreement between the contractor and the policyholder.

Reviewing the Estimate

Before you sign a construction contract, be certain that all of the necessary work is included and described. If you sign a contract that reads "Repair all fire damage for $50,000," you are giving the contractor license to do the work in any manner he chooses. Sometimes an estimate will be based on a scope of work, and this will be so stated in the bid. This is sufficient if the scope of work is detailed and complete. If not, additions or clarifications may be necessary. If the scope of work is actually an itemized estimate, it should be thorough as well. Carefully go over the work, and see to it that the estimate specifies exactly what is to be done. If the estimate includes replacement of paneling in a specific room, and you expect birch veneer, write in the words "birch veneer," and initial the notation. This will serve to reduce the possibility of disputes once the work is underway.

If you are going to consider any alterations or changes in materials, you will want a fully itemized estimate. In many cases, an itemized estimate will include a separate price for each part of the job, right down to the last strip of molding. There might be a separate price for replacing a door, replacing a light fixture, carpeting a room, and painting it. Minimally, you will want individual prices for each repair, broken down by individual categories. This means separate prices for roofing, painting, carpet, etc. If you want to make an alteration when installing cabinetry, for example, it will be difficult for you to do so unless you know how much was included in the cost to repair for cabinetry. It is not critical that an estimate be itemized in any particular manner. As long as you are able to determine individual prices so that you can calculate the potential savings when considering variations on reconstruction, the itemization is sufficient.

Payment Assignments

Usually before repair work begins, the policyholder is asked to sign a document called a "payment assignment," "payment authorization," "authorization to pay," or "direction to pay." This document gives the company the right to make the contractor a named payee on the payment draft, and is requested by the contractor for the contractor's protection. Unless the policyholder signs a payment assignment, the insurance company does not have the right to include the contractor's name on the draft. This is because the insurance policy contract is between the company and the policyholder, and the contractor is not privy to the contract. If the company names a third party on the draft without the authorization of the policyholder, it is not really complying with the contract. The only time a company can rightly pay a contractor direct is when it hires the contractor. In most states, mortgagees are named on all insurance drafts, based on policy endorsements that are required by state law.

Payment assignments can sometimes work to the advantage of a policyholder, because if a contractor is to be named on an insurance draft, the contractor may be willing to start work without a down payment. At the same time, the policyholder is protected as the draft cannot be cashed by the contractor until signed by the policyholder.

Penalty Clauses

A penalty clause stipulates that the cost of a job decreases by a given amount each day that the job exceeds the completion date written into the contract. It is usually difficult to get a contractor to commit to a completion date and include a penalty clause in a contract because contractors usually have several jobs going on at one time. There also may be forces beyond contractors' control, such as labor strikes, material availability, etc., that can cause delays. In a situation where time is of the essence in completing repairs, you can always try and get the contractor to include a penalty clause in the contract to avoid unnecessary delays.

In Sum

When compiling a claim on a dwelling or other structure, keep in mind:

- The four steps to compiling a claim are:
    1) Determining coverages
    2) Determining the scope of repairs
    3) Determining the cost to repair
    4) Determining the amount of the claim
- Always consider possible variations on reconstruction—they can make the difference between a large out-of-pocket expense and a satisfactory claim settlement.
- Overhead and profit allowances are part of the cost to repair, and should be part of the claim payment whether a contractor is involved in the repairs or not.
- Building code requirements are a factor in most reconstruction projects, but a creative approach will usually keep them from being a problem.
- Dealing with contractors is another factor in most reconstruction projects, and assertiveness on the part of the policyholder is usually the key to a positive outcome.
- Be sure that all of the work you want done is included in the estimate, and in the construction contract.
- Payment assignments may enable you to negotiate favorable financial terms with a contractor, if used creatively.
- Penalty clauses can be used to avoid delays in construction projects, although most contractors resist using them.

10 What's Involved in Personal Property Claims

• Depreciation on Personal Property • Presenting Your Claim • Documentation • Mysterious Disappearance and Conversion • Keeping an Inventory • Additional Living Expense Claims • An Example

COMPILING a personal property claim is similar to putting together a dwelling claim. There are specific matters that need to be considered, though for the most part the four steps described in chapter 9 relative to building claims can be followed.

The first thing to do is determine what personal property is covered. The exclusions in the policy that refer specifically to personal property, as discussed in chapter 4, may be relevant. The "special limits on certain property" may be a factor as well. If the claim is a theft claim, the exclusions that apply to theft may come into play. As in the case of a dwelling claim, it is necessary that the issue of your coverage be resolved before the claim is compiled and submitted.

The second step is to establish the scope of the loss. This means determining what property is going to be included in the claim and preparing a personal property inventory. You should always complete an inventory on your own; this task should not be left to the insurance company representative. It is sometimes difficult to determine if damaged items are to all practical purposes destroyed or if they are cleanable, especially in the case of fabric items such as furniture, clothing, and draperies. If such a question comes up, it is common practice for a company to pay for cleaning with the understanding that the property will be replaced if the cleaning operation is unsuccessful. Determining the scope of a personal property loss is seldom a cut-and-dried affair, and there are usually several points of discussion.

The next step is to establish the replacement cost of the property included in the claim. Again, you should do this with every item, even though it involves a substantial amount of work. It will be the company representative's job to check your prices and to dispute them if necessary. Obviously, it will be contrary to your interest to get your replacement cost prices from discount or low-priced stores. Always keep a record of your price references so that your prices can be substantiated if they are questioned.

The last step is determining the actual cash value amount of the claim. This is necessary in most cases as the replacement cost coverage on personal property usually requires replacement of the property involved before the difference between the actual cash value and the replacement cost is collectible. In other words, you will have to purchase a new chair before the company will pay the full amount for the chair that was damaged beyond repair. This is another area that will involve negotiation as it takes into consideration depreciation on your personal property.

Depreciation on Personal Property

Depreciation is another favorite term of insurance companies; it refers to the concept that an item becomes less valuable as it wears out or is used up. Depreciation is used to calculate the actual cash value of personal property, which is based on replacement cost less depreciation. The amount of depreciation that applies to an item is based on the ratio between the life expectancy and the age of the item. For example, a five-year-old refrigerator with a ten-year life expectancy may be depreciated 50 percent.

Most insurance company representatives use depreciation tables to calculate depreciation on personal property; however, to strictly adhere to such tables is inaccurate. The amount of use, abuse, and wear and tear on property varies considerably. A quality piece of furniture of traditional styling, for example, will depreciate slowly in the home of an elderly couple and rapidly in a home occupied by a family with nine children. It might be appropriate to base depreciation on effective age—which considers the real amount of wear and tear on an item and the effective remaining useful life—as opposed to actual age. Insurance companies sometimes consider these criteria when they apply.

If the actual cash value of personal property was established on the basis of market value as opposed to replacement cost less depreciation, settlement amounts on such claims would drop drastically. As an illustration, consider the example of a simple dress shirt. Let us assume we have a shirt that cost $30 new and is a year old. We will assume a three-year life expectancy, which indicates 33 percent depreciation per year. The actual cash value of the shirt, then, is about $20. How does this compare with the market value of such an item? Look at the cost of used clothing in secondhand stores; the shirt might sell for $2. The difference we see in this example approximates 1,000 percent!

In many cases, claims personnel do consider obsolescence as a factor in personal property claims, and this is appropriate to a certain extent. An item that is subject to changes in fashion or technology can rightfully be seen to depreciate faster than an item of classic style or enduring design. A classic blue blazer would depreciate more slowly than a designer leather jacket that will be in style for only a year or two. Similarly, an 8-track tape deck might have a lower value than a cassette deck of the same age and quality, because of the relative obsolescence of 8-track stereo systems. However, the consideration of obsolescence in the case of personal property claims is touchy as it points to market value as a criterion for value, as opposed to replacement cost less depreciation. It is evident that some people surround themselves with obsolete or out-of-style things, and such property is certainly valuable to them until it wears out.

It is appropriate for a company to consider market value in the case of personal property that has exhausted its useful life as stipulated in the depreciation tables. For example, if you include a fifteen-year-old television set in a claim, and the set was in working condition at the time of loss, the company cannot take the position that the set had exhausted its expected useful life, was living on borrowed time, and had no value. They would be responsible to respond to the value of the set based on market value. It is also proper for market value to be used to establish value relative to items that do not depreciate, are irreplaceable, or actually appreciate with age. This category includes antiques, silver, jewelry, fine art, and other such property. Although market value might be a proper criterion for valuation in these cases, it is not appropriate at other times, and the actual cash value of personal property should be based on replacement cost less depreciation.

The following chart indicates a general rate of depreciation per year for common household items.

Household Item	Rate of Depreciation
Major appliances	8 to 10%
Minor appliances	10%
Wool blankets and beds	5%
Rugs	10%
Clothing	33%
Jackets and coats	20%
Suits, sweaters, etc.	25%
Draperies	10%
Furniture	10%
Athletic gear	10%
Luggage	5%
Musical instruments	10 to 15%
Office machines	10%
Eyeglasses	10%
Kitchen utensils	5%
Power tools	5%
Hand tools	0 to 5%
Toys	25%

Remember, these figures are general guidelines, and the actual amount of depreciation contemplated is always negotiable.

Presenting Your Claim

Once you have done the work involved in the four steps outlined at the beginning of this chapter, presenting your claim is relatively simple. You will have determined coverages, established the scope of your loss, calculated the replacement cost of the involved property, and estimated the actual cash value of each item included. Your personal property that is not covered, or is in excess of a limit, should be contained in a separate section so that you will have a firm and separate figure for presentation to the company. This amount will also represent an uninsured casualty loss for tax purposes.

Your personal property claim should take the form of a personal property inventory. Inventory forms are frequently given to policyholders by company personnel for completion. The forms usually have several columns on them and include space for such information as a description of the item, the place purchased, the date purchased, the replacement cost, the amount of depreciation that applies, and the actual cash value of the item. Your inventory, when submitted to the company, should include: a description of the item, the age of the item, the replacement cost, the amount of depreciation that you feel applies, and your estimate of the actual cash value of each item regardless of the information requested in the form provided by the company. If there is no space on the form for depreciation or actual cash value figures, make space for them or draw up forms of your own.

Total each page of the inventory separately and sign each page. The last page of the inventory should include two grand totals. One will be the *amount of the loss,* which will include all property damaged, covered or not, and will be based on actual cash value or replacement cost, whichever method of valuation applies. The second grand total will be the *amount of the covered property,* and will not include property that is not covered or is in excess of a limit, and will again be at actual cash value or replacement cost, whichever method of valuation applies. If replacement cost coverage applies, also include an actual cash value figure for the covered property, as this will establish the amount of the initial payment and the amount of the pending replacement cost claim. Documentation should be attached separately. It is sometimes helpful to number the items in the inventory and to note the applicable number on the respective pieces of documentation attached.

Your inventory represents your determination of the loss

and your demand to the company. It is a place to begin negotiating and should be viewed as an opening offer. Your claim should not be inflated but should not be artificially low, either. The prices in your inventory will probably be checked by the company representative, and the value figures may be adjusted as well. The representative's figures should not be seen as gospel carved in stone but should be considered a counteroffer. This is a highly negotiable area of the adjustment, and you will want to reach an agreement acceptable to both you and the company representative. If it is not possible to reach a mutually agreeable figure with the company representative, and you desire to pursue the matter further, your rights of recourse lie in the appraisal process, which is discussed in chapter 12.

Documentation

The Standard Fire Policy requires the policyholder to submit to the company all bills and invoices that substantiate a loss. It is your obligation as a policyholder to support your claim as thoroughly as possible and to submit all available documentation to the company. Bills, invoices, receipts, cancelled checks, warranty cards, instruction booklets, box labels, family photos and the like can be used to demonstrate ownership, age, and value of the items included in your claim.

Sometimes claims personnel request that policyholders attempt to obtain copies of original invoices from retail outlets on larger items included in a claim, and although it is inconvenient for a policyholder, it is the company's right to make such a request.

What if documentation is simply not available? A lack of documentation can throw a shadow of doubt over an insurance claim and may lead a claims representative to speculate that certain property included in the claim never existed. It is not uncommon for some adjusters to diminish the payment on such property substantially. Many people disagree with this practice.

Companies do have the right to require that all available documentation be submitted; but in the absence of available documentation, they must assume that their policyholders are honest and will act in good faith in the absence of concrete evidence to the contrary. Unless evidence of fraud is present, the company is obligated to respond to a claim in full.

One effective course of action in such a situation is to obtain affidavits from friends attesting to the fact that you owned the property in question and that it was what you say it was, and supporting your position in general. An affidavit is simply a written statement signed by the individual preparing it. It can be handwritten in any manner desired, preferably by the person giving the affidavit.

Mysterious Disappearance and Conversion

While we are on the subject of personal property claims, it is necessary for us to look at two causes of personal property losses that are not covered by most homeowners policies: mysterious disappearance and conversion. Frequently, policyholders expect losses by mysterious disappearance and conversion to be covered because they are closely related to theft losses; there is only a fine line between the two. For this reason, it is important that these two concepts be discussed in detail.

Mysterious disappearance is the disappearance of property from a known location during a known period of time under baffling or curious circumstances. As mysterious disappearance is not one of the named perils that apply to personal property, loss by mysterious disappearance is not covered. Nor does coverage apply to property that is merely "lost." Mysterious disappearance cannot contain the element of possible theft.

If such a possibility can be demonstrated to a reasonable degree, it can be argued that the loss in question is the result of theft and is therefore covered. The homeowners policies state that the definition of theft includes the loss of property from a known location when a probability of theft exists.

Two examples of mysterious disappearance are:

A woman is vacationing in Los Angeles with her husband. She leaves a shopping plaza and walks with her husband a half mile or so to their hotel. Upon arriving at the hotel, she realizes that her watch is missing. She remembers that the watch was on her wrist at the shopping center as she checked the time. It is evident that the watch was "lost" between the time she left the plaza and arrived at the hotel, although she has no idea what happened to it. Had the woman left the watch on a sink in a restroom and returned some time later to find it missing, a probability of theft would exist, and the woman would have a valid theft claim.

The insured, a construction worker, has two wristwatches. One is an inexpensive digital watch that he wears every day, and the other is a gold-plated quartz watch that he wears on special occasions. On returning home one evening after a night on the town, he removes his good watch and places it in a drawer with the rest of his jewelry. Upon looking for the watch several weeks later, he notices the watch missing and cannot find it anywhere. If a claim were filed for the watch, it might well be denied. In the absence of a probability of theft (which might exist if there had been a large party at the house), the loss would be the result of mysterious disappearance.

Another cause of loss to personal property that is similar to theft, yet is not covered by homeowners policies, is conversion.

Conversion is essentially a nonfelonious abstraction of goods—a wrongful exchange of goods from one person to another. Conversion can also be defined as intentional interference with personal property that deprives the owner of use of the property. Conversion can include: (1) maintaining possession of goods in order to coerce the owner into an action; (2) refusing to give property to its rightful owner; (3) misuse of property for a specific purpose (your mechanic using your car to qualify for the demolition derby); or (4) intentional damage to or alteration of property. Two examples of loss by conversion are:

A homeowner enlists the services of a contractor to perform repairs at his residence. After completing part of the job, the contractor attempts to raise the price of the job. The homeowner refuses to pay the additional amount. The contractor, out of spite, removes some of the homeowner's personal property, and essentially holds it for ransom. The policyholder claims that the items have been stolen. The company would probably deny the claim on the grounds that it is the result of loss by conversion.

Another policyholder, a rich physician, enlists the services of a housekeeper to do housework and care for his children. While the policyholder is absent from home, the housekeeper thoroughly cleans out the entire premises and hauls the goods away in the policyholder's car. The policyholder claims that the personal property taken by the housekeeper is stolen. Again, a claim of this kind might well be denied on the grounds that it is the result of loss by conversion.

Unfortunately, there is not much that a policyholder can do to get an insurance company to pay for a loss by conversion. Such losses are simply not covered under most homeowners policies. Since conversion is a somewhat vague concept, it can sometimes be argued that a loss is the result of theft, and not conversion, which would obligate the company to pay the claim. This approach may prove difficult, however, and may also involve dealing with legal concepts beyond the scope of the average homeowner's expertise.

Keeping an Inventory

The most important factor to remember in regard to personal property is to keep a property inventory. The primary value of an inventory is that in case of a severe loss, you will have a detailed list of your property and will not have to trust to your memory to compile a complete inventory. If you think that you are able to remember accurately what property is in your home, give yourself a test: pick a drawer, a closet, or other isolated part of your house. Try and remember the items contained in that location. Then go and look. You will be amazed at the number of items you have forgotten.

There are several methods of taking an inventory available to you. You can go through the house and photograph your property. You can complete a written inventory or walk through your home with a tape recorder and verbally record in detail what you possess. There are also video taping services that will record your possessions on video tape. Whatever method you choose, keep the inventory away from home in a safe place, such as a safe deposit box at the bank.

Taking photographs is probably the simplest, most effective method of taking an inventory of your personal property. First take some overall photos of each room. Photograph each wall, the items on the walls and on all of the shelves and dressers in the room, etc. Photograph the rugs on the floor if they are valuable. Then take close-ups of all of the valuable items. If there are distinguishing marks on some of the things, like a signature on a painting or print, be sure that it gets into the picture. Open drawers and closets, and photograph the contents. If the items are cluttered together, spread them apart, or take them out and spread them out on the floor or on a table.

When photographing china, silverware, stamp and coin collections and things of that nature, take care to see that each item is photographed. You might take a picture of an entire set of silver flatware, for example, and then take a close-up of one of the pieces to record in detail the kind of silver it is and the details of the pattern. After the pictures are processed, go through them carefully to ensure that all of the items photographed are clear. Make sure everything important is included. Then record all pertinent information about the items on the back of each photo. Indicate the manufacturer's name, the style and model number if applicable, and any other necessary information. This kind of detailed photographic record of your property will be of tremendous value if the property is severely damaged.

Additional Living Expense Claims

At this point, we have learned how claims should be compiled on dwellings and other structures and personal property. The subject of additional living expense coverage has been discussed, but we have not yet examined what is involved in actually compiling a claim for additional living expenses. We will do that now.

Compiling an additional living expense claim is relatively simple. It is merely a matter of comparing your normal expenses against the expenses incurred during the period your house or apartment is untenantable. The expenses considered should include mortgage payments, utility bills (electricity, gas, water, telephone, etc.) food, laundry, temporary housing, moving, storage, etc.

When you are forced to live in a temporary residence following a loss, your mortgage payments obviously continue, and your rent at the temporary location is an additional expense over and above your normal mortgage payment. Similarly, meals in restaurants cost more than meals eaten at home, and food costs over and above your normal food budget are an additional living expense. Other expenses, such as heating and light bills, will be less during the time the dwelling is being repaired. This too must be considered.

List all of your "normal" expenses, including those referred to above. Compile a total that will apply to the projected period of untenantability. These figures can be based on past experience, and the time involved can be estimated for the purposes of the claim, projected to the anticipated completion date for repairs. Then, list all expenses you expect to incur during the time you will be displaced from your home. This list will include all of the items in the list of normal expenses, some of which will be lower than normal or may not apply at all (utilities, for example), and some of which will be higher (food, laundry). Also include all additional living expenses, such as rent, moving, storage, etc. The difference between the two is your additional living expense claim.

An additional living expense claim can be estimated and included in its entirety in the total claim, even though the dwelling is not repaired and it is not possible to secure a completion date. This will ensure that necessary money is available to pay your mortgage, rent, and other bills when they are due. It should be easy enough to get the company to agree to consider a supplemental additional living expense payment if the expenses are incurred because repairs take longer than expected.

Here again it is necessary to document your claim as well as possible. Save all receipts and invoices so that your additional living expense claim can be thoroughly substantiated.

An Example

Now that we have gone through the steps of how a dwelling and personal property claim should be handled by the policyholder, let us look at a scenario of how it all works:

Our [fictitious] case involves Frank Hall, an electronics engineer living in the Silicon Valley near San Francisco, California, his wife, June, and their two children: David, an active, athletic boy of twelve, and Janet, a bright, spry, mischievous little girl of seven. The fifth member of the family is a wiry golden retriever we shall call Sparky.

The Hall family lives in a four-bedroom, one-story ranch-style home, nestled in a quiet, woody hillside neighborhood in Cupertino, California. The house is about thirty years old, has a shake shingle roof, wood siding, and is in good condition. There is a two-car garage attached to the house.

It is Friday evening, and Frank and June are going to drive into San Francisco and see a play. David is off at summer camp, and Janet is going to have a friend over to spend the night. A neighbor's teenage daughter will baby-sit.

All is quiet most of the evening, with Janet and her friend playing in Janet's room, and the baby-sitter watching TV in the den. The two girls decide to pretend they are camping and proceed to make a tent out of a blanket in the bedroom closet. Naturally, Sparky is enthusiastically participating in the operation, although he is more trouble than he knows. Candles removed from the dining room table are lit to provide authentic flickering firelight. Hungry after setting up camp, the adventurers hike off to the kitchen for a store of provisions. Sparky follows, and his flailing tail knocks over the candles on his way out of the tent. The girls are way ahead of him and do not notice.

The candle flames ignite some paper bags and shoeboxes on the floor of the closet, and the fire creeps up to the blanket used for the tent, then to the clothes in the closet. The flames soon burn out of the open closet door to the bed and adjacent end table. As the girls return, arms loaded with peanut butter, crackers, and milk, they are met by thick smoke and flames leaping out of the bedroom.

As it turned out, the baby-sitter got everyone out safely and ran to a neighbor's with the children. By the time the fire department arrived and extinguished the fire, it had burned for over twenty minutes. Flames had burned through the closet wall to the kitchen and the dining room. The fire also jumped through the door to the garage, which had been left open so that Sparky could get out, and into the living room, where the damage was minimal. The fire burned out of the bedroom door to the pass and entry hall and into the den. The two bedrooms at the end of the hall were heavily damaged by smoke, although flames never reached them. The roof was two-thirds destroyed when the flames burned through the bedroom ceiling.

Needless to say, the family stayed in a motel that night, and the insurance company hired a security guard to watch over the house. The day after the fire, Frank and June removed all of the usable things that they needed on a day-to-day basis from the house, as well as the valuable items. Sparky was put in a kennel. Two days following the fire, Mr. Hall met Jim Johnson, claims representative for Acme Insurance Company, and Bill Williams, of Do Rite Construction Company, at the house. Together they walked through the premises, assessing the damage and discussing the scope of repairs.

It was apparent that most of the roof was gone, and they decided that nothing would be gained by trying to save any of it. The entire roof structure would be replaced. The ceiling joists over 50 percent of the structure were damaged and were included in the scope. Fire had damaged the structural members in the wall between the bedroom and the exterior and in the partition walls in the kitchen and bedroom. About sixty feet of interior partition wall was earmarked for replacement. The scope included all of the Sheetrock in the bedroom, kitchen, dining room, pass and entry halls, den, and garage. The Sheetrock on the ceiling in the living room was included as well. The acoustic ceilings throughout the house were to be resprayed, and the carpet was to be replaced. Mr. Johnson wanted to consider shampooing the carpet in the two rear bedrooms, but Frank argued that the carpet was continuous throughout the house and the new carpet would not match the old. Johnson agreed to include the carpet in the bedrooms.

Electrical repairs were included, specifically all of the fixtures in the severely affected rooms and the wiring throughout the house. Interior finish items were also considered, including doors, windows, trim, paneling, paint, and the cabinets, flooring, and other finish items in the kitchen. It was determined that a portion of the exterior siding would have to be demolished and replaced in order to replace the framing in the wall between Janet's bedroom and the exterior.

At this time, Frank raised the questions of coverage and betterment. He was told that the carpeting would be subject to depreciation, as would the built-in stove and dishwasher. The refrigerator, which is not built in, is a personal property item, and would be included in the personal property claim. He was also told that there would be a certain amount of electrical work necessary to meet the latest building code regulations, but that it would be difficult to determine just how much until the building inspector had seen the job.

Frank asked Johnson what he would do about getting repair estimates, and Johnson said that he intended to request bids from Do Rite and one other contractor that he knew, and that the claim would be concluded based on the lower of the two bids. This told Frank that he did not need to worry about getting estimates for submission to the company, as the matter would be resolved on the basis of Johnson's estimates anyway. Frank asked if Acme would hire the contractor or if that responsibility would be left to him. No, he was told, Acme did not want to get involved in the construction business. Frank would be left to hire the contractor.

Frank and Johnson reviewed the personal property in the house and agreed that there was nothing to be saved in any of the rooms affected by the fire. The property in the den and other two bedrooms appeared potentially salvageable, and Johnson told Frank to have the clothing items dry cleaned and to save the receipts. Most of the furniture in the den was ruined by smoke, but the items in the bedrooms looked as though they could be saved. Johnson called in a contents cleaning company, which took the salvageable items to a warehouse to be cleaned and restored.

Johnson instructed Frank to inventory the destroyed property in great detail. He gave Frank printed forms on which to list every item damaged in the fire. They discussed the family's living situation, and Johnson explained that it would take at least two months to rebuild the house and that the family should find an apartment or rent a house to stay in while the repairs were underway. Yes, the company would pay the deposits and credit them against the claim, as they are returnable. Frank was told to save all the receipts for expenses, including meals, laundry, etc.

In the days that followed Johnson's visit to the premises, Frank asked his broker and his friends for referrals to contractors experienced in fire restoration work, and talked to several. He was unimpressed with most of them, but finally found one he liked who agreed to look at the house. Frank met with Al Bryre, of Basic Builders, the next day. Frank went over the scope of repairs with Bryre in detail and discussed possible alterations that could be made. Frank requested that Bryre wait until hearing from him further to put together an estimate.

Several days later, Frank got a call from Johnson, who told him that the estimates had been received. Williams's was the low bid, with the cost to repair $48,000. Frank asked Johnson to send him a copy, and it was received the next day.

Frank took the time to categorize the prices in the estimate by trades, and the breakdown looked like this:

Demolition	$ 2,500
Carpentry labor	8,000
Carpentry materials	4,000
Sheetrock	4,200
Electrical	2,000
Vinyl flooring	800
Heating	1,200
Formica	1,100
Cabinetry	2,400
Plumbing	800
Roofing	5,500
Paint	3,200
Janitorial	500
Appliances	1,400
Carpet	2,400
Subtotal	$40,000
+20% profit and overhead	8,000
Total	$48,000

Johnson stated that he would apply $600 betterment to the appliances and $900 betterment to carpeting. He stated he could not pay the profit and overhead on the amount of the betterment, so an additional $300 would be subtracted from the cost to repair. This meant a total reduction for betterment of $1,800.

The revised replacement cost amount was $46,200. The $250 deductible would also apply, so the most that could be collected was $45,950.

At this point, Frank tried to find out how much the additional electrical code work would cost. Johnson was not able to tell him, and Williams said he would have to talk to the electrical inspector before he knew for sure. Frank requested that he do so as soon as possible, and Williams reluctantly agreed. A few days later he had the answer; the electrical code work would run $1,200.

All of this meant that if Frank hired Do Rite to repair the house, he would have to pour $3,250 of his own money into the job. It was either that or consider just what kind of repair job he could get for the $45,950 the company was willing to pay.

Frank called Johnson and discussed this problem with him. Frank asked if there would be a problem of any sort collecting the amount of the replacement cost claim if he did not rebuild the house exactly as it had been. Johnson stated yes, there might be if any of the alterations were considered improvements to the property. Frank informed Johnson that he needed a definite answer to the question and a response in writing before he could decide just what approach to take. Frank told Johnson that he did not feel it was the company's position to monitor the repairs, and that as long as the money paid was spent restoring the property, the company was liable to respond to the full cost of the work up to $45,950. Frank followed up this conversation with a letter in which he stated the question might have to be referred to legal counsel for review, if not satisfactorily resolved. He requested a written response within one week. A few days later, the letter arrived. Acme Insurance Company would pay the replacement cost claim, provided Frank could demonstrate that the money was spent on the reconstruction.

The first thing Frank did was call Bryre and ask him to bid the job just as Williams had. Because he wanted to see how the two compared, he did not tell Bryre what Williams's price was, or even that he had Williams's bid. When Bryre sent in his bid, Frank learned that his price was higher than Williams's by $4,000.

At this point, Frank and June began seriously to consider potential alternative repairs and look for ways to save on the cost to repair. They discussed alternative roofing materials with several roofers and found that there were modern composition materials available that were made to look like shake shingles, were very attractive, and cost about 40 percent less than shake. Moreover, the composition material lasted as long as shake and was far less flammable. Frank remembered that a friend of his had recently had his house repainted by a fireman who did painting on his days off. He got the number of the man and called him for an estimate. The cost, he was told, would be $2,560, a 20 percent savings over the painting subtotal in the Do Rite bid. Frank also noticed that carpet was included in the Do Rite estimate. He reasoned that he did not need the assistance of a general contractor to arrange to have carpet installed in his home, and decided to purchase the carpet himself and save the contractor's overhead and profit. Frank also decided he did not really need to replace the Sheetrock in the garage, and decided to omit that part of the work altogether.

Frank then called Williams and proposed the changes on the roof, paint, carpet, and Sheetrock. Williams said that he had no objection to omitting the paint and carpet from the estimate, but that he would rather be responsible for the roof himself. However, he agreed to use the composition shingles Frank wanted and the lower price. Williams also agreed to reduce the cost of the job by $800 if the Sheetrock in the garage was omitted.

At this point, Frank knew that the alternative repairs he was considering were feasible and knew that even if he could not negotiate a lower price with either Williams or Bryre, he could save enough to have the repair work done for the amount of the claim. The subtotal on roofing would be reduced by 40 percent, a savings of $2,200. He would not have to pay profit and overhead on the saved amount, which would further reduce the price by $440. He would save $640 on the paint, plus the profit and overhead on Williams's paint price, which would be another $640. An additional $480 would come from saving the profit and overhead amount on the carpet, and the total savings on Sheetrock, including profit and overhead, would be $960. The total savings, then, would be $5,360. This meant that Frank now had an additional $2,110 that he could spend on alternative repairs.

He and June began to think about the changes they would make. They decided to install ceramic tile on the kitchen counter instead of Formica and to upgrade the kitchen cabinets to a better grade of hardwood.

Frank and June had always talked about installing skylights in the roof above the kitchen and den but had never done so because of the trouble and expense. They decided they would have skylights installed if they could get them included for the amount of money they had available.

Frank went to both Williams and Bryre with the proposed changes and got prices from them. Williams agreed to make the changes in the counter and cabinets and to include the skylights for the additional amount of money involved. Bryre was also willing to consider the changes, but his price was still higher than Williams's. Frank asked Williams for some references, inspected a couple of jobs that Do Rite had done, and talked with the customers. Satisfied that Do Rite was a reputable company and that its work was of high quality, he awarded it the contract.

During the time that Frank had been working on the building claim, he and June had been working on the inventory of personal property as well. They spent hours each evening in the house, listing each item damaged, trying to remember how long they had had it and where it had come from. After the inventory was completed, they began the arduous task of determining replacement cost values; catalogs were consulted, stores were visited, and phone calls were made. Depreciation was calculated based on expected life, age, and condition, and an amount of claim on personal property was established.

At last they found a rental house available for a short duration and cleared the cost with the company. After Frank and June rented the house, the salvaged property was moved from the cleaning company facility to the rental house. Some furniture was rented to replace items destroyed in the fire until replacement property could be purchased. Slowly, surely, and laboriously, the family settled down in their new quarters while putting their home back together.

Eventually the house was repaired, and they moved in. They bought new furniture, draperies, and other items. It had been a trying experience, filled with confusion, questions, worries, and inconvenience. It had also been a lot of work. But it had all been resolved in the end, and they were a happy family. The new kitchen was delightful, and the skylights were a welcome addition. With the house refurbished, things once again settled into peace and tranquillity.

In Sum

When considering what's involved in personal property claims, keep in mind:

- Compiling a personal property claim is similar to compiling a building claim—the same 4 steps outlined in chapter 9 can be followed.
- The concept of depreciation is highly relevant to personal property claims, and is based on the ratio between life expectancy and the age of the item.
- The format in which your claim is presented is important, and a well-presented claim will make for a quick settlement.
- Documentation is another important aspect of personal property claims, and you have both rights and obligations in this area.
- Loss by mysterious disappearance and conversion are not covered under many homeowners policies.
- An inventory of your personal property will enable you to file a complete claim in the event of a severe loss.

11 Friends and Foes

- *Public Adjusters* • *Mortgage Companies* • *The Insurance Commissioner* • *Lawyers* • *The Internal Revenue Service*

THE field of homeowners insurance is broad in scope, and there are many different professionals involved in the business. You will undoubtedly deal with some of them whether you are buying insurance, filing a claim, or arranging to have repairs made to your house. Some of these individuals will turn out to be friends and some foes. Let us have a look at some of these specialists and the jobs they fulfill.

Public Adjusters

Public adjusters are insurance adjusters who act on behalf of policyholders in filing property claims. They are licensed by the state in which they operate, either under the same license used by an independent adjuster working for insurance companies, or, in some states, under a separate license designed especially for them. Because of the nature of the business, most public adjusters work exclusively for policyholders and not for insurance companies, even though their license might allow them to do both.

Public adjusters go after business on their own. They learn about fires and other incidents involving loss of property primarily by listening to the radio transmissions of the fire departments in their area. They typically have a scanner in the office that is closely monitored by day and a second set at home. If information about a fire is obtained soon enough, a public adjuster will usually drive to the location immediately and attempt to locate the owner of the damaged property, which might be a building, or business or personal property. If the owner cannot be located, county records, newspaper articles, or other sources will be used to determine the identity of the owner of the property involved, and contact will be made with the owner as soon as possible. The field of public adjusting is highly competitive in large metropolitan areas, and the smart public adjuster knows that the policyholder must be found as soon as possible if there is to be a chance of signing the owner up for representation.

Upon locating the owner of the damaged property, the public adjuster will attempt to get the owner to sign a contract. The contract, which may be called an assignment of interest or something similar, stipulates that the public adjuster will represent the policyholder in filing the claim and will require the insurance company to make the public adjuster a named payee on the payment draft. This contract can sometimes be cancelled by a homeowner within a matter of days after its execution, as required by homeowners protection laws that apply in some states. If you have a question about this, you should contact the insurance commissioner's office in your state.

The public adjuster's sales pitch usually centers around his experience and expertise in the area of insurance claims and may well contain words of warning about the problems that might be encountered in dealing with an insurance company. At times, public adjusters neglect to inform prospective clients that a fee is charged for the service provided, and the policyholder might wrongfully be led to believe that the public adjuster is a city, county, or state employee. The hours following a major fire or other disaster can be unsettling, to say the least, and at such a time a homeowner might be upset and unable to listen carefully to misleading implications made by unscrupulous public adjusters.

All public adjusters charge a fee for their work. The fee is universally based on a percentage of the amount of the paid claim. The percentage figure used varies, and is usually determined by the size of loss and the potential for realizing and justifying a large fee. The fee amount ranges from as low as 3 percent on very large commercial claims to a maximum of 15 percent or so. The average range is about 7 to 10 percent. (One public adjuster in California was found to be leaving the amount of the fee out of the contract altogether, settling the claim with the company, hiring a contractor to repair the damages, and keeping the balance. It is thought that his fee might have been as high as 50 percent in some cases.) In most instances, the fee is based on the amount of the entire claim, including additional living expense claims, even though the public adjuster might not do any work to negotiate or settle this part of the claim. Some public adjusters realize that this may not be fair to their clients and base their fee on an appropriate percentage of the building and personal property claim amounts alone. Needless to say, the public adjuster's contract should always indicate clearly the exact basis for the fee charged, and all alterations of the contract and other agreements should be in writing.

Once the policyholder is signed up, it is the public adjuster's responsibility to act as an agent for the policyholder in filing the claim with the company. There is, however, usually nothing in the public adjuster's contract that spells out the duties required, nor anything to specify or guarantee the amount of the settlement. The involvement on the part of public adjusters in claims varies to a great extent. Some do not assist in the time-consuming physical work involved, thus leaving the policyholder to make an inventory of damaged property, research prices, etc. Other adjusters will put on their coveralls and roll up their sleeves and participate earnestly in the process, working long, hard hours. A good public adjuster will assist the policyholder in finding temporary living quarters and in getting settled after a severe loss. Most public adjusters have contractors write building repair estimates for them instead of putting figures together on their own. The contractors are sometimes paid for the estimates; sometimes the bids are submitted free of charge because of the potential job that might come to the contractor.

Ultimately, a public adjuster's activity on a given claim might be limited to signing up the policyholder, calling a contractor for an estimate, reviewing and perhaps adjusting an inventory prepared by a policyholder, and negotiating a quick settlement with the insurance company. This may involve just a few hours of work. When we consider that a public adjuster's fee on a $50,000 loss may approximate $5,000, it is apparent that a public adjuster can make a substantial amount of money for a minimum amount of work.

This setup can also inspire a public adjuster to settle a claim for a relatively low figure instead of fighting for a higher settlement. A quick settlement means quick money, and 10 percent of a bird in the hand might be better than 10 percent of a slightly bigger bird in the bush. Obviously, such an attitude will not effectively serve a policyholder's interests, yet there might be little to be done about it after the fact short of suing the public adjuster. A settlement made by a public adjuster might actually be higher than one made by a policyholder alone although this can never be known. It can never really be determined that the public adjuster's involvement resulted in a higher payment.

Some public adjusters, like insurance company adjusters,

work to see that the damaged building can be repaired for the amount of the payment made by the company, and may become involved in negotiating the cost to repair with a contractor and seeing that the policyholder is getting a good deal on the repair job. This means more work for the adjuster, and it also means a more complete and valuable service to the client. Most public adjusters, however, merely negotiate settlement of the claim with the company, collect their fee, and walk away from the problem.

When a policyholder hires a public adjuster, it is possible that a competitive relationship will develop between the public adjuster and the company representative. To an extent, this competitiveness may have a sound basis. The company adjuster knows that a claim submitted by a public adjuster may well be inflated; this is how most public adjusters justify their fees. The company representative may have to negotiate rather aggressively in order to bring the claim amount down to an acceptable level.

It is well known that many individuals working in the field of property claims harbor a distaste for public adjusters, and it is when emotional resentment becomes a factor that serious problems may develop for a policyholder. As an example, imagine that a company adjuster who does not like public adjusters obtains a bid from a contractor that is certain to be very low. The resulting settlement would be artificially low as a result, and the policyholder would ultimately pay the price because he would not be able to get the necessary repairs completed for the amount of the payment. Unfortunately, some company claims representatives are willing to overlook the undue burden placed on the policyholder in such a situation in order to make things difficult for a public adjuster. Furthermore, contractors sometimes collaborate in these efforts, either implicitly or explicitly, because the involvement of a public adjuster in a claim frequently means a loss of business to the contractors who count on insurance companies for their livelihood.

It is further relevant to note that hiring a public adjuster can work against a policyholder in still another way. A policyholder cannot be expected to adhere to and understand the various policy provisions. An insurance company and the courts will sometimes be very lenient in this regard. But if the policyholder is represented by a public adjuster, the policyholder's representative is seen as an expert by the insurance company and the courts. As a result, failure to comply with policy provisions may have more serious consequences for the policyholder. In any event, it is probably safe to say that a public adjuster will not be granted the benefit of the doubt by an insurance company or by courts of law as readily as would a policyholder.

When considering the value of public adjusters to the consumer, we see that there are benefits as well as liabilities. One of the benefits is that if a policyholder is having trouble with a company when filing a claim, it might be advantageous to have access to expert assistance. However, public adjusters are more valuable to business than to the average homeowner. In a business, a large commercial loss may be extremely complicated and a public adjuster's expertise may be desperately needed by management. If the assistance of a public adjuster suits your needs, it is always prudent to research the reputation of the firm you sign with.

Mortgage Companies

Most homeowners have a mortgage on their home. All of the standard homeowners policies contain a mortgage clause that requires the insurance company to name the mortgage holder on payment drafts. The reason for the clause is simple: to protect the mortgagee's interest in the property.

An individual or firm holding a mortgage on a piece of property has a vested interest in seeing that the property is secure and kept in good repair. If the property is damaged and the owner abandons it to the note holder, there is the certainty of the headache that accompanies foreclosing on the property and a very real possibility of financial loss. For example, assume that a home worth $100,000 is half owned by the homeowner and half owned by a mortgage company. Each party has an interest of $50,000 in the house. Further assume that the house is damaged by fire, and the cost to repair is $75,000. If the homeowner were to receive the entire payment and abscond with the money, the mortgage company would be left with a piece of property worth $25,000 and an unpaid loan of $50,000. A loss of $25,000 to the mortgage company would result. The mortgage clause in the homeowners policy is intended to guard against this kind of situation.

In spite of the sound reasoning and good intentions behind the mortgage clause, it can serve to cause problems for policyholders when a claim is paid, as the mortgage company has control of the funds, and the funds are then not available to the policyholder to use in repairing the damaged building. Most mortgage companies are easy to deal with in this respect and will release part of the money, but if it chooses, the mortgage company can hold on to all of the funds until all repairs are completed before releasing the money. This can make it hard for a policyholder to make partial payments to a construction firm doing the repair work. In such a case, the homeowner is left to finance the construction work out of his own pocket or through whatever channels are available. The fact that the property, though damaged, might be worth more than the amount of the loan may not convince the mortgagee to release funds. Lending institutions are in the business of making loans, not buying and selling distressed real estate. The bank simply does not want the headache of foreclosing and repossessing the property. In these kinds of cases, it is common for policyholders to use their own personal property payments to finance repairs. This is a hardship on the homeowner, but it may be necessary if the mortgage company involved is uncooperative.

In the case of damaged property that is not kept "in good repair," the mortgage company may have the right to call the loan, which means that it could require payment of the loan in full upon demand. This can sometimes be the case even though the loan payments are made on time. The potential problem here is obvious as the policyholder would have to refinance the property elsewhere, which would surely be an inconvenience and a hardship. A mortgagee usually retains the right to repossess property that is not kept in good repair, even if payments are properly made.

Another potential problem is that in a situation where a mortgagor defaults on loan payments, the mortgagee might have the right to apply all or part of the insurance payment toward payment of the loan. This is a rather difficult thing to do legally, yet can be used as a threat to get a policyholder to finance a reconstruction project so that the mortgage company does not have to release any funds.

The mortgage company is never entitled to hold more money than the amount remaining on the loan, and must release the balance to the policyholder. In some cases, it may prove wise to merely pay off the mortgage if the balance is small, thus assuring that all necessary funds are available to pay for repair work.

Haggling with a mortgage company might well be a trying and tedious task, and there is usually little to be done to get a mortgage company to release funds if it does not want to. This is not to say, however, that the actions of the mortgage company are not to be questioned. Mortgage contracts vary considerably, and it is always prudent to examine the agreement on your own and to hire legal assistance if necessary. Also, since a lot might depend on decisions made by a specific loan officer, it usually helps to negotiate with the loan officer in an amicable manner.

In a situation where a mortgage company refuses to release funds prior to completion of repairs, the problem can sometimes be solved by negotiating a payment schedule with a contractor that will eliminate the need for the policyholder to finance the construction work. In spite of what any one contractor might say, there is absolutely no rule about how a contractor is paid for repair work. Some construction firms are willing to finance smaller projects and will not require any payment until all work is completed. In the case of larger projects, however, at some point all contractors require partial payments, and that point varies based on the capital the contractor has available at the time to finance the work and the extent to which the contractor is willing to absorb the cost of doing so. Keep in mind that the cost of such financing is always considered by the contractor, and if the contractor is to finance the job to a significant degree, the overall cost of the repair work will probably be higher as a result.

In some cases, a contractor might request a deposit up front, perhaps as much as one-third of the job cost, before work begins. This is wholly unsatisfactory, as it results in a considerable hardship on the customer. It is also illegal in some states. A more typical and reasonable deal might call for payment of one-third of the contract price upon completion of demolition and delivery of materials, one-third upon completion of all rough work, and the remaining one-third when all of the finish work is done. A solvent contractor of any respectable size should be willing to finance $10,000 to $20,000 worth of work at any given time. Requests of partial payments of less than $10,000 might be a tip-off that the firm you are dealing with is too small to be safe and might be in a poor financial position or have a poor credit rating, or it might just be that all of a company's capital is tied up and not available to finance your job. A large, financially secure firm might routinely finance jobs of $50,000 or more without requiring partial payments. But as pointed out, the price, as a result, will be higher. Remember that the payment schedule in a construction contract is always negotiable, and if you cannot reach a satisfactory deal with a contractor, look for another one.

Before signing a construction contract, check with your mortgage company to see what kind of deal will be satisfactory to it and negotiate your construction contract accordingly. Keep in mind that the mortgage company will usually have the property inspected before releasing any funds, which will take time. Most contractors will wait patiently for this to be done, although others might complain about the delay. Payment assignments, described in chapter 9, can be helpful in this area. If a contractor knows that he will be named on a draft and that the money is available, he may be more willing to begin work and continue it without partial payments.

If the contractor you select carries the job entirely, it does not matter if the mortgage company holds all of the funds. However, if partial payments are required—and they usually are—it is important to assure the contractor that he will be paid. At times, a mortgage company may refuse to release funds, arguing that the work completed does not justify the amount of the payment. But most reputable companies will release the money as a gesture of good faith as long as the mortgagor is working to repair the property.

The Insurance Commissioner

Each state has an insurance commissioner. Most are appointed by the governor of the state, although some are elected officials. The insurance commissioner's office is given the task of monitoring the activities of insurance companies, assuring proper compliance with state laws regulating insurance companies, and making certain that the companies are solvent. One of the main jobs of the commissioner's office is to see to it that policyholders are treated fairly. If you have any kind of question or problem regarding insurance in general or a claim in particular, the insurance commissioner's office is available to offer information and assistance. The staff of an insurance commissioner's office is usually knowledgeable and will probably be able to answer questions about the appropriateness of the actions of your insurance company.

If you are involved in a claim and you feel that the company's position on a particular issue might not be correct or that you are entitled to treatment different than that afforded by the company, you can look to the insurance commissioner's office for guidance and assistance. At times, questions can be answered by phone. Most offices prefer that inquiries be submitted in writing. The office may send you a form to fill out and return, and that form will constitute a formal inquiry.

The commissioner's office will then investigate the issue. This usually involves contacting the company and finding out what it is doing. If the office of the commissioner feels that the company's actions are improper, it will recommend that the company handle the matter differently. Technically, the insurance commissioner's office has the ability to revoke the company's license, although this is almost never done because it would mean causing problems for many innocent policyholders. So in effect, the commissioner's office cannot force the company to comply with its recommendations. Most companies, however, respect the insurance commissioner's office, and the input provided by the office is given some weight.

In sum, the insurance commissioner's office is a highly valuable and powerful avenue of information and recourse for the consumer. As a source of information, it is invaluable. The office is not only knowledgeable but also impartial. Furthermore, if there is a problem with your claim, the commissioner's office can be a powerful force.

Lawyers

It is not difficult to imagine a situation occurring where it will be prudent, if not necessary, for you to obtain legal advice on a claim. Merely handing your case over to a lawyer, however, can often be counterproductive. When the matter in question is a property insurance claim, there are several things to keep in mind.

Like public adjusters, lawyers frequently make or justify their fees by squeezing more money out of a claim. In the case of an accident claim, this works well for a lawyer as the lawyer may well be able to get a client more money than the company would initially offer if the claimant was not represented. This is primarily a result of the relative nature of the damages and the potential outcome of litigating the case. Because a lawyer knows that a higher settlement will result from litigation, and because the insurance company knows that litigation will cost several thousand dollars, the threat of litigation may rightfully lead the insurance company to pay more on the claim. By contrast, in the case of property claims, it is often difficult for a lawyer to increase the amount of the payment because of the concrete nature of the damages. The cost to fix a building or replace a personal property item can be well established, and the policy does not cover consequential losses, such as pain and suffering, so such things do not enter into the picture.

To illustrate this distinction, let us look at two hypothetical cases. The first scenario presents a typical conversation between an adjuster and a lawyer regarding settlement of a liability claim arising out of a slip-and-fall accident. We shall say the facts are that the lawyer's client received a broken leg when he fell down on the policyholder's front porch, and the policy-holder's insurance company has admitted liability and has agreed to pay the claim in full. We will assume that the claimant (the person making claim against the homeowner's insurance company and who is the injured party) was offered a settlement for bodily injury based on medical expenses, lost wages, physical therapy treatments, with something thrown in for general damages, such as pain and suffering. We will assume that the offer for settlement is $1,000 for fixed costs, such as medical bills, etc., and $500 for general damages, such as pain and suffering. Our claimant is unhappy with the settlement (probably because he has been told by friends of pots of gold at the end of the settlement) and hires a lawyer. The first conversation between the lawyer and the company adjuster might go something like this:

LAWYER:	My client feels that your offer of $1,500 is entirely too low, and I agree with him.
ADJUSTER:	Well, his special damages are only $1,000, and we're paying all of those, and we're also throwing in $500 for general damages. We feel that ours is a generous offer.
LAWYER:	Well, you know treatment is not necessarily complete. My client may need to continue physical therapy and medical treatment for a while yet. We don't know how the injury will heal. And besides, $500 for general damages is ridiculous. This person is losing the use of his leg for six months. He can't play on his softball team and can't do any backpacking this summer, not to mention the general discomforts he will endure. I think the generals should be at least $5,000.
ADJUSTER:	We aren't willing to pay $5,000. There just isn't that much involved here to justify such an excessive payment.
LAWYER:	Well, if we can't get a satisfactory settlement out of this case, we'll just have to go to court. Now we don't want to do that, and I'm sure you don't either, because you know it will cost your company several thousand dollars to litigate this case. So in the interest of getting this thing resolved, we might be willing to settle for $4,000.
ADJUSTER:	Can't do it. It's just too high. Allowing for the worst, the case might be worth $2,500.
LAWYER:	Look, my time is valuable and so is yours. Let's agree on $3,250, split the difference, and wrap this one up.
ADJUSTER:	Fine. I'll put the release in the mail today.

Because the adjuster knew that it would be expensive to litigate the case, and because he knew that the award by the court would probably be more than he had offered, it was obviously in the best interests of the insurance company to pay a little more and get rid of the claim. This is justifiable not only in view of the expense of litigation, but because of the subjective value of pain and suffering and other damages constituting general damages. How much is a season on the softball team worth?

Let us look at another example that refers to a building claim. The insured in this case submits an estimate to the company higher than the company's contractor's estimate. The insured wants the company to pay based on his contractor's estimate and not the company's, and the company refuses. Angry, the insured hires a lawyer. The first conversation between the lawyer and the company adjuster might go something like this:

LAWYER: My client tells me that he submitted a repair estimate to you for $40,000, and that you're only willing to pay $30,000.

ADJUSTER: That's correct. We have an estimate from Acme Construction that includes all the necessary work for $30,000.

LAWYER: Well, my client doesn't like Acme Construction. The guy was arrogant and rude when he came out to meet my client, and therefore the settlement offer is not satisfactory.

ADJUSTER: Your client doesn't have to have Acme Construction do the work; we don't care who does it. However, we cannot justify a payment greater than $30,000, because we know that the house can be repaired for that.

LAWYER: Well, look. If we can't get this resolved in a satisfactory manner, we'll just have to sue you.

ADJUSTER: Sue us for what?

LAWYER: Bad faith.

ADJUSTER: We haven't acted in bad faith.

LAWYER: Well, you know that the litigation will cost money, and I'm sure you don't want to incur a lot of legal fees.

ADJUSTER: You're right, we don't. But we still can't justify paying an additional $10,000 on this claim because the guy from Acme Construction was arrogant one day. As long as he'll do the work for the amount of our offer, we can't pay more.

LAWYER: I'm going to talk to my client about this, and I'll get back to you.

ADJUSTER: Fine. I'll look forward to your call.

In the interest of fairness, it should be said that the threat of litigation might carry some weight in the adjuster's mind, because insurance companies do sometimes respond to this kind of blackmail. Also, a good lawyer would probably be able to come up with some substantial arguments for a higher payment, perhaps based on changes in the scope of repairs or questions on coverage. But you will notice that the company is going to be far less likely to respond to the threat of litigation in the case of a property claim than in a case of a liability claim, and this is primarily because of the concrete nature of the damages. In this case, the lawyer might not be able to get the client any more money as a result of his involvement, and the lawyer's fee might have to be paid from the original settlement amount.

The foregoing example illustrates the danger of hiring a lawyer to represent you in filing a property claim. You will have to pay the lawyer's fee no matter what, even if the settlement is not increased by the lawyer. Most lawyers are anxious to take over the case altogether and handle it all the way; you should think carefully about this before making such a commitment. The solution to this problem is merely to seek advice from a lawyer and pay only for that advice. It might be worthwhile to pay a lawyer to write a letter to an insurance company in some cases, as such a letter might get results that your own letter would not.

If you do hire a lawyer to become involved in a property claim, it is an absolute must that you hire one who specializes in property insurance matters. The average lawyer on the street might be fully capable of handling a personal injury case and probably does more of that than anything else. But a lawyer who does not make property insurance a specialty may not be familiar enough with the intricacies of the field to represent you effectively. Many lawyers are willing to take a case even though they may not know enough to handle it properly. They may feel that merely threatening litigation will be enough to resolve the matter satisfactorily and may know just enough to be dangerous to your cause.

The Internal Revenue Service

The fact that you file an insurance claim may be something that should be considered on your tax return. As a taxpayer, you are allowed to "write off" certain losses. These losses include those not covered by insurance, or portions of losses that are not covered. For example, if your insurance company paid you only $500 for a $5,000 emerald-cut diamond ring that was stolen, you would be entitled to a $4,500 write-off. The law does not, however, allow deductions for losses that would be covered by insurance but were not claimed. As an example, if you had a $400 pair of skis stolen and your deductible was $250, you could not write off the $150 amount over your deductible if you decided not to file a claim because the loss was too small.

As is typical with the IRS, there are rules that apply to such deductions. There are three primary rules to keep in mind. First, you can only deduct the amount of your uninsured casualty loss over $100. In the foregoing example of the diamond ring, the write-off would be $4,400. Second, you cannot write off the part of the loss that the insurance company had paid for. Third, the IRS will want you to base your deduction on the lower of two amounts—the original cost of the property or the market value. If the ring had been purchased for $1,000 and had appreciated to a value of $5,000, the IRS would want you to use $1,000 as a value, subtract the $500 paid by the company, then the obligatory $100 deduction, and write off $400.

As of 1983, the tax law allows a deduction for uninsured casualty losses only when the amount of the deduction exceeds 10 percent of your adjusted gross income. This is a significant change over the old law: previously, you could deduct your entire uninsured loss. You may also deduct the cost of appraisals incurred after a loss; they are a valid "miscellaneous deduction." For additional information about how tax laws apply to casualty losses, you can write to your local IRS office for IRS publication #547, *Tax Information on Disasters, Casualties and Theft.*

In Sum

When thinking about friends and foes, keep in mind:

- Public adjusters are insurance adjusters who act on behalf of policyholders in filing claims.
- All public adjusters charge a fee for their work, and the service they provide for that fee varies.
- In most cases, a mortgage company will be involved in a reconstruction project, and as a result issues may come up that must be addressed by a policyholder.
- The position of a mortgage company on a particular issue is not above question: mortgage contracts will frequently point out the proper course of action.
- Your state insurance commissioner's office is a terrific source

of information, and can intervene on your behalf when questions come up on claims.

- At times, lawyers become involved in insurance matters, but care must be taken to see that the lawyer's involvement is justifiable.
- Tax laws contain provisions that apply to insurance claims—be aware of them.

12 Knowing Your Rights

• Policy Interpretation • Established Policy Interpretations • Fluctuating Interpretations • Third Party Negligence • Proximate Cause and Concurrent Causation Theory • Appraisal and Suit • Subrogation • Unfair Claim Settlement Practices Acts • Fair Treatment • Salvage • Statements • Nonwaiver Agreements • Reservation of Rights Letters • Cancellation

Policy Interpretation

Knowing your rights under any policy you have is of prime importance. To know these rights, it is necessary to understand how policies and/or policy language is being interpreted in the courts today. "Policy interpretation" refers to the act of determining what coverage the policy provides in a practical sense, in spite of what it says or appears to say. A court's interpretation of specific policy language will always be made within the context of the policy—because a policy is a contract. The court will consider all of the case law that applies. For this reason, a court's interpretation may well differ considerably from that of a layperson's reading of the policy. The subject of policy interpretation is immense; thousands of questions have arisen, and thousands of cases have been tried. A discussion of even some of them would fill volumes. The thing to remember is that the policy may not mean what it appears to mean to you.

This is not to say that a policyholder's interpretations and expectations are to be ignored by the courts. In fact, one judge stated, "When someone purchases standard fire insurance, he does so with the idea in mind of protecting himself and his property from loss or damage. Our decision conserves that expectation." In another decision, coverage was provided for damage to personal property even though that coverage had not even been included, as the policy was written only to cover the building. The court found that the policy form used contained references to personal property coverage although the coverage had to be separately purchased. The policyholder argued that because the form included references to personal property, it was reasonable to expect that it applied. The court ruled that this was logical thinking, and the insurance company had to pay for a personal property loss even though it never received any payment for the insurance. After that ruling, companies were required to see to it that the policies specifically indicated that personal property was excluded when such was the case.

Established Policy Interpretations

To illustrate how correct policy interpretation works, let us look at a couple of examples. The policy excludes damage caused by "water which backs up through sewers or drains."

Taken at face value, this would appear to apply to a backup that originates in any drainage system, such as a sink drain. This would also seem to include overflow of a rain gutter, which might cause rainwater to run down an exterior wall, through a window, and inside the dwelling. Although there might be some variation from jurisdiction to jurisdiction, in most cases both of the causes of loss mentioned would be covered. It has been established in the courts that this policy exclusion applies only to drains that are off the insured premises. The intent of the exclusion in the policy is to prevent an insurance company from having to pay for backups caused by an overflow of city or county sewer or drainage systems because such a loss might affect many policyholders in a given area and would be contrary to the concept of insurance.

Consider another interpretation of coverage. Homeowners policies also exclude loss of gold and silver by theft. If an expensive gold fountain pen was stolen, one might think that the gold exclusion would apply, but it does not. The gold and silver items excluded must be given their value by the fact that they are gold or silver, and an item with a primarily utilitarian function, like a pen, would not meet such a criterion. Therefore, the gold fountain pen would be covered for loss by theft. Another policy interpretation example might be the exclusion that applies to business personal property away from the premises. It might appear that any personal property used in one's business would fit the definition of excluded property. In fact, only property that is exclusively business property is excluded. A professional photographer's camera equipment would be covered, for example, if he or she used it to take family photos.

Fluctuating Interpretations

Insurance policy interpretations change with time as courts decide coverage questions. An illustration of the fluctuating nature of policy interpretation and the way that case law on insurance questions is established by the courts concerns the rule about the exclusion of money in the homeowners policies and how it applies to coin collections. Initially, the homeowners policies excluded loss of money caused by theft, and insurance companies typically applied this exclusion to coin collections. However, it was a position frequently questioned by policyholders, and in 1967 a New York court ruled that coin collections were commodities in themselves, separate from money used as a medium of exchange. This set a precedent requiring companies to pay for stolen coin collections. When they drew up policy forms, the policy underwriters had intended to exclude coin collections, but because of the vagueness of the policy language the exclusion was not upheld by the court.

Interestingly, in a later case, a policyholder tried to collect for stolen coin collections under a commercial crime policy, arguing that the collections were money and not a separate commodity. The case was decided for the policyholder, although the decision did not affect the precedent already established in regard to the homeowners policies. The court based its ruling on the fact that the policies were ambiguous and vague and therefore should be interpreted against the maker of the contract in both cases.

Some questions of policy interpretation are based on theory and principle more than on specific policy language. An example of this kind of question might be the distinction between "friendly fires" and "hostile fires." A friendly fire can be defined as a fire intentionally lighted and confined to its intended place. A hostile fire might result if a friendly fire exceeded its intended boundaries. The classic example of a friendly fire is a fire in a fireplace. Damage caused by such a fire by burning an object nearby or burning an object thrown into it might not be covered under traditional thinking. However, if a log from a fireplace were to roll out onto the floor, the fire would be seen to exceed its boundaries and would then become a hostile fire. Even though the policy does not address this issue at all, it is a long-standing principle that only damage by hostile fires is covered; damage by friendly fires is not. The rationale is that if a fire was intentionally lighted, as a friendly fire is, it would not be accidental and would not comply with the fundamental principle of insurance that losses be accidental.

Many recent cases revolving around this theoretical question have changed this long-standing principle and in effect have weakened it. It has been argued that damage to an object tossed into a friendly fire is covered because the fire was not intended to burn the object involved. In other cases, heat or smoke emitted from a friendly fire has damaged nearby property, and it has been argued that such a loss is covered. In one case, a commercial oven was left on all night and became severely overheated because there was nothing in the oven to absorb the heat. Even though this is a perfect example of damage caused by a friendly fire, the court required the insurance company to pay the claim because the policy was seen to be ambiguous, because the loss was "unanticipated" by the insured, and because the policyholder expected the loss to be covered. This is a good example of the modification of coverage provided by insurance policies in an instance where the lay person might not have any indication of the changing doctrine or of the issue itself.

Third Party Negligence

Before concluding the subject of policy interpretation, let us look at a recent trend in the area of homeowners insurance that has affected the industry in a highly significant way. This is the question of third party negligence as a covered peril under all risk homeowners policies.

As stated previously, the principle behind an all risk policy dictates that damage by any cause is covered, except those excluded. In chapter 4 we have reviewed the exclusions that apply. There is, however, no reference in the exclusionary language to improper construction, design, installation, or other problems caused by the negligence of a third party. The following is an example of one such hypothetical loss:

Assume that a house is designed by an architect who hires a soil engineer to draw up the specifications for the grading and foundation work around the house. Assume, too, that after the house is built, severe rains cause saturation of the ground the house is built on, causing the earth to sink and the house to shift on its foundation, and ultimately resulting in considerable damage to the structure.

It might appear that the cause of loss in this case would be earth sinking or earth movement, both of which are excluded perils. If the cause of loss were traced back to the heavy rains, the cause might be flood or surface water, which are also excluded. But what if it is determined that the engineer, architect, or builder made some sort of error or poor decision or was merely ignorant of the potential difficulties his work might produce, and it was this that caused the problem? The cause of the loss might then be attributed to the negligence of the person or firm responsible for design or construction. And such a cause of loss is not specifically excluded. So even though there might be several perils involved that are excluded, the fact that the initial cause of the loss can be traced back to third party negligence may indicate coverage.

The court decisions on these kinds of third party negligence cases essentially state that the insurance company has ample opportunity to limit coverage in the policy to whatever extent it desires and has not excluded improper design or construction or third party negligence. In a nutshell, the upshot of recent court decisions was that if the exclusion is not clearly spelled out in the policy, it simply does not apply. For years, however, these kinds of claims were denied on the grounds that they were not the results of fortuitous losses or because they were the results of certainties. This position recently has been weak-

ened by the courts, because these long-accepted principles are
not clearly spelled out in the contract.

The absurd although logical extension of this thinking contains awesome possibilities. A great many causes of damage
can be traced back to some kind of lack of vision or judgment,
if not to actual negligence. The most farfetched scenario resulting from this thinking involves a class action suit brought by
the inhabitants of an area suffering a major earthquake who
demanded payment on the grounds that the buildings were
not built strongly enough to withstand the earthquake and
placed the blame on the designers, builders, or the city buildings
departments that approved the plans. In fact, some companies
are contemplating paying for earthquake damage claims at
this time partly because of the possibility of claims being filed
based on the third party negligence argument. Such an event
would surely bankrupt the companies writing insurance in the
area of a major earthquake. There is some speculation that
this phenomenon may cause many companies to simply stop
writing all risk policies if the trend continues in its present
direction. As a result of the recent erosion of exclusions in
all risk policies, it has been suggested that insurance companies
merely write a policy without exclusions and charge a higher
price for the product. Some modern policies now contain specific language that excludes loss by faulty construction or certain
kinds of third party negligence.

It is obvious that there are aspects to policy interpretation
and coverage questions that are simply unknowable to the
average policyholder. The layperson is not going to be familiar
with all of the intricacies of the field or with the current trends
and laws. This does not mean that it is necessary to run to a
lawyer with every little question on coverage. It merely means
that questions that do come up need to be carefully addressed
and researched. Again, the answer is to talk to as many people
as possible, including the insurance company and whomever
else you can find who may have a knowledge of the matter
at hand.

Proximate Cause and Concurrent Causation Theory

Like the friendly fire/hostile fire principle, the insurance industry and courts have supported what is known as the "rule of
proximate cause" for years. Essentially, the proximate cause
is a factor or cause that sets into motion an unbroken chain
of events. By way of example, consider a loss where wind
blows down a large tree, causing the root system to move
the earth around it and the earth movement to topple a retain-
ing wall. The courts have traditionally ruled that if the proximate
cause of a loss is a covered peril, then the entire loss is covered
even though excluded perils may come into play during the
sequence of events. The damage to the wall then would be
covered even though the actual damage was caused by earth
movement, an excluded peril. Because the peril of wind is
covered, and wind is the proximate cause of the loss, the entire
loss is covered.

In contrast, the rule has always maintained that if the proximate cause of a loss is not covered, the entire loss is not covered
even if a covered peril comes into play by way of an unbroken
chain of events. An example of such a claim might involve
earth movement that ruptures a water line. Water damage
caused by a ruptured plumbing pipe would normally be covered, but if the proximate cause of such a loss was earth movement, an excluded peril, then the loss itself would not be covered under traditional thinking based on the proximate cause
rule.

If you look at the section of the homeowners policy outlining
exclusions, you will see that this principle is specifically contra-
dicted—to an extent—by policy language. The policy states
that fire ensuing from an excluded peril is covered, although
only the damage by fire is covered and not the damage caused
by the excluded peril. This rule is also altered in another portion
of the homeowners policy, as damage due to loss of refrigera-
tion is covered, but only if there is damage to the equipment
on the premises by a covered peril. Vehicle damage to a power

line next door resulting in loss of power to a refrigerator unit, for example, would not be covered even though the proximate cause rule says it would.

Recently the proximate cause rule has been changed by the "concurrent causation theory." The theory holds that whenever a covered peril interacts with other perils, covered or not, there is coverage for the loss regardless of where the covered peril fits into the sequence of events. This doctrine is fairly well rooted in California law, and stems from a series of cases. One of the most significant involved a homeowners policyholder who had modified a handgun. The handgun had accidentally discharged while lying in a moving vehicle injuring a passenger in the car. Initially, the insurance company denied liability coverage on the grounds that the loss was the result of operation of a vehicle that had been driven over rough terrain. The court ruled that the modification of the gun was also a cause, and that the insured was negligent in modifying it. The company was required to pay the claim.

Concurrent causation theory is also a consideration in the case of earthquake claims. The policy covers building collapse but not earthquake. The argument is that since both things happen concurrently, the resulting damage is covered. Clearly, there is a difficult question to answer about the interaction of the two perils. And if insurers cannot demonstrate that the entire loss was caused by earthquake and not collapse, they may be treading on thin ice in denying such claims. Indeed, in one case the court stated that it was the duty of the insurer to demonstrate that the cause of the loss was an excluded peril and that there was no interaction with covered perils. The combined effect of the third party negligence peril argument and concurrent causation doctrine is causing most companies to look very carefully at earthquake claims, and many are merely paying them rather than risk the huge punitive damage judgments that might result from denying them. Here again, it is evident that the underwriters intended to exclude

loss caused by earthquake, even loss contributed to by earthquake, yet court decisions are undermining that intent. Some
modern policies include language intended to counteract some
of the effects of this doctrine.

Appraisal and Suit

Another area in which policyholders are frequently unaware
of their rights is when questions of appraisal and suit arise.
The policy provisions referring to appraisal and suit are contained in the Standard Fire Policy. The provisions are highly
consistent from state to state, as the Standard Fire Policy is
used in its original form in most states. There is, however,
minor variation in the language in some states.

The section of the Standard Fire Policy that addresses the
issue of appraisal is commonly called the appraisal clause.
Appraisal is a means by which disputes over the value of damaged property or the amount of a loss can be resolved. Appraisal is not intended to be used to resolve questions of coverage; only questions about the amount of a company's liability
can be considered.

In the event of a dispute over value, a policyholder is required
to go through the appraisal process before filing suit against
the company for failure to pay the requested amount. The
policyholder agrees to this condition when executing the policy.

The standard appraisal clause reads as follows:

*In case the insured and this Company shall fail to agree as
to the actual cash value or the amount of loss, then, on the
written demand of either, each shall select a competent and
disinterested appraiser and notify the other of the appraiser
selected within twenty days of such demand. The appraisers
shall first select a competent and disinterested umpire; and
failing for fifteen days to agree upon such umpire, then, on*

*request of the insured or the Company, such umpire shall be
selected by a judge of a court of record in the state in which
the property is located. The appraisers shall then appraise the
loss, stating separately actual cash value and loss to each item;
and, failing to agree, shall submit their differences, only, to
the umpire. An award in writing, so itemized, of any two when
filed with this Company shall determine the amount of actual
cash value and loss. Each appraiser shall be paid by the party
selecting him and the expenses of appraisal and umpire shall
be paid by the parties equally.*

Note that either the company or the policyholder can demand appraisal. In theory, this gives both parties to the contract
equal access to the arbitration process. The typical policyholder,
however, is not even aware of the appraisal option and probably
would be hesitant to use it in any event because going to
appraisal means jumping into highly unfamiliar territory. The
truth is that the process is not as difficult or treacherous as
it might seem; it is in fact rather simple.

The first requirement is to demand appraisal in writing. The
second is to select an appraiser. Both are simple enough steps
to take. The demand letter need only be clear and understandable and need not fit any particular form. Many times the
demand letter will name the appraiser selected by the party
demanding the arbitration. Nor should selecting an appraiser
be difficult. If the dispute involves a particular kind of property,
the appraiser should be an expert in that area. If building damages are involved, the appraiser can be a contractor, an architect, or a construction cost consultant. If the property included
in the claim covers a broad spectrum, then an adjuster, public
or independent, would be a good bet. Here again, your agent
might be able to offer suggestions in this area. Attorneys specializing in insurance work will also usually be able to suggest a
good appraiser. Each party must select his appraiser within
twenty days of demanding appraisal or receiving the demand.

The appraisers then attempt to select an umpire. This can be an expert of some kind if a specific kind of property is in question, or a retired judge, or other disinterested party. If the appraisers cannot agree on an umpire in fifteen days, the umpire is chosen by a court. The appraisers then attempt to agree on the value of the individual items in the claim, and differences between them are resolved by the umpire. The outcome of the appraisal becomes the basis for payment of the claim. Each party pays for his own appraiser, and the two share the cost of the umpire equally.

The entire appraisal process involves three things. Demanding appraisal, appointing the appraiser, and paying the appraiser and umpire. The first two things are easy. The latter may involve a lot of money, especially if the appraisal is complicated or if there are numerous items involved. This factor will obviously offset any increase in recovery and should be considered before demanding appraisal.

In most cases, an appraisal award will be in between the policyholder's demand and the company's settlement offer. After the appraisal process is completed, either party can sue the other if dissatisfied with the outcome of the appraisal. It is up to the dissatisfied party, however, to accept the burden of proof in setting aside the appraisal, and in the absence of evidence of wrongdoing or incompetence, this will be hard to do. It is also expensive.

Some companies demand appraisals in order to coerce policyholders into accepting a settlement offer. The average homeowner will be frightened by an official and ominous-sounding letter demanding appraisal and requiring the appointment of an appraiser within twenty days. This is a rather rare practice and is somewhat less than scrupulous as policy provisions should not be used to threaten an unwary policyholder. The fact remains, however, that if appraisal is demanded by a company, the only choices available are settlement or appraisal. Remember, though, that you can still negotiate the settlement upward or downward after receiving the appraisal demand letter, and there is nothing to require blind acceptance of the company's offer.

The homeowners policy requires that a suit against the company be filed within one year after the date of loss, and also stipulates that the policyholder must comply with all of the provisions of the policy before suit can be brought. This means that the policyholder must go through the motions of filing a claim as outlined in the policy before filing suit. First, it would be necessary to file a proof of loss, as required. If the claim was denied, the policyholder could then file suit on the issue of coverage. The only time a policyholder can sue a company on a question of value, without first going through the appraisal process, is when the insurance company refuses to go to arbitration.

Subrogation

Another important area in which you should be aware of your rights concerns the question of "subrogation." Subrogation is the substitution of one party in place of another party in respect to a claim or lawful right. If your property is damaged by a negligent party, you would have the right to recover from him for the damage. If the insurance company pays you for the loss, the company takes over the rights of recovery previously belonging to you. The principle of subrogation evolved to prevent injured parties from collecting from both the insurance company and the responsible party.

The policy provisions regarding subrogation are contained in the Standard Fire Policy, and the policyholder is required to assign all right of recovery to the company. The company also has the right to argue cases in court under the policyholder's name instead of the insurance company's name. This is because the company feels that the court or jury will look more favorably on a "little guy" than a large corporation.

If you sustain a covered loss caused by a negligent third party, the insurance company must pay the claim on a timely basis. It cannot simply tell you to seek recovery from the responsible party. Sometimes a company will stand aside and allow a third party or insurance carrier to compensate a policyholder, but this can only rightfully be done with the consent of the policyholder. The company would have to pay the claim promptly if the policyholder requested that it do so. After the claim is paid, your insurance company will try and obtain restitution for the damages from whomever caused them. As an example, if your home was damaged by a vehicle, your company would pay to repair the damage, and would then try to get the owner of the car, the driver, and/or its liability carrier to pay it back.

Your insurance company can only seek recovery from a negligent third party on your behalf if the insurance company has made a payment to you. The company cannot go against a responsible party on your behalf if the damages are not covered. Furthermore, your company can only seek recovery in the amount of its financial interest in the claim, which is the amount paid to you. The insurance company will also ask the responsible party to pay the amount of your deductible, which will be returned to you. It goes without saying that your company cannot try to get you recovery for consequential or uncovered losses.

If your property is damaged by a third party, you have the choice of trying to get payment from the responsible party or filing a claim with your own insurance carrier. If the responsible party readily admits liability and is willing to pay for your damages, it might be satisfactory to accept payment from him. This course of action can sometimes turn into a rough and rocky road. You might get assurances that "things will be taken care of" immediately following an accident, whereas getting paid might be another matter entirely.

Also, keep in mind that delayed reporting of the claim might result in difficulties later on. Sometimes you can notify your company of the claim, tell it that the responsible party is taking care of it, and that you will file a claim against your policy only if necessary.

There are two primary advantages to collecting directly from the responsible party as opposed to collecting from your insurance company. The first is that it will improve your claim record. But since you carry insurance to protect yourself against loss, this benefit may be of limited value. The second advantage is that you may be able to collect for consequential damages that your company would not pay for. This would include property not covered by your policy or other damages, such as loss of use of your property, lost wages, etc. Also, you would not have to pay your deductible. The liability of a responsible party or a liability insurance carrier goes beyond simple property damage and extends to damages of a more general nature.

Conversely, there are advantages to allowing your company to make payment to you and then have it go against the responsible party for reimbursement. First of all, your insurance company fights your battle for you. It will make demands to the responsible party, and its legal staff will become involved if necessary. Also, you may well get your payment more quickly from your own company than from a responsible party or liability carrier. This may mean getting your property repaired faster as well. In addition, once your company has fought the battle of demonstrating liability on the part of the responsible party, you would be able to step in and ask for restitution for your consequential and uncovered losses.

One point to keep in mind is that in the case of smaller claims, your insurance company may not work very hard to recover from the responsible party. In such a situation, you will want either to check on your company's progress with subrogation periodically to make sure something is being done or to handle the matter yourself. Your company is not in any way required to pursue subrogation recovery for you to recover your deductible or for any other reason.

Let us look at an example that will illustrate the workings of the subrogation recovery process and the options and complications involved:

Imagine that your neighbor's children are playing with matches next door, and they accidentally ignite a small fire that burns your wood fence and smokes up one side of your house. You indicate to your neighbor that you feel that he is liable since his children started the fire, and he reports the matter to his homeowners carrier. His insurance company determines that the loss was an accident and assumes liability. In such a case, it might be to your advantage merely to accept payment from your neighbor's insurance carrier and not to bother filing a claim of your own. This way, you would not have to pay your deductible and would be able to collect for consequential losses, which in this case might involve lost wages if you had to leave work as a result of the fire.

Assume, however, that there are several children involved, and it is difficult to pinpoint the child responsible. You could potentially wait for months for all of the parents and their insurance companies to investigate the incident and take a position on liability. In all probability, the inconclusive facts would lead the companies to take a conservative position on liability. In such a case, you would want to collect from your carrier directly and let your company collect from the responsible parties if possible. Then you would be able to continue the pursuit of your claim against the responsible parties for consequential losses or other damages not paid for by your company.

Simply stated, if liability is clear against a party, collecting from him may be quick and easy. If the facts are muddled and liability is unclear, a long, complicated investigation may result, and you would be better off to collect from your company.

Needless to say, you cannot rightfully collect from both your carrier and the responsible party. If you do collect from the responsible party after your company pays the claim, you are obligated to return the money to your insurance company.

Unfair Claim Settlement Practices Acts

To further protect your rights, most states have now adopted Unfair Claim Settlement Practices Acts, which are laws passed by state legislatures to regulate the behavior of insurance companies in respect to the payment of claims.

In 1973 California became the first state to pass into law the Model Unfair Claim Settlement Practices Act, as proposed by the National Association of Insurance Commissioners. Other states quickly followed suit. The model act was revised in 1975, and this version became the standard for most of the Unfair Claim Settlement Practices statutes now in existence. The statutes primarily regulate the treatment of policyholders and claimants. The requirements are usually not more than a couple of pages long and are usually clearly written and easily understood. The content of these statutes varies from state to state although most are similar in actual requirements. A copy of the Unfair Claim Settlement Practices Act that applies in your state can be obtained from your State Insurance Commissioner's Office.

The California version of the Unfair Claim Settlement Practices Act is fairly representative of the statutes in general and is included here as an example.

Section 790.03(h)—*Knowingly committing or performing with such frequency as to indicate a general business practice any of the following unfair claims practices:*

(1) Misrepresenting to claimants pertinent facts or insurance policy provisions relating to any coverage at issue.

(2) Failing to acknowledge and act reasonably promptly upon communications with respect to claims arising under insurance policies.

(3) Failing to adopt and implement reasonable standards for the prompt investigation and processing of claims arising under insurance policies.

(4) Failing to affirm or deny coverage of claims within a reasonable time after proof of loss requirements have been completed and submitted by the insured.

(5) Not attempting in good faith to effectuate prompt, fair, and equitable settlements of claims in which liability has become reasonably clear.

(6) Compelling insureds to institute litigation to recover amounts due under an insurance policy by offering substantially less than the amounts ultimately recovered in actions brought by such insureds.

(7) Attempting to settle a claim by an insured for less than the amount to which a reasonable man would have believed he was entitled by reference to written or printed advertising material accompanying or made part of an application.

(8) Attempting to settle claims on the basis of an application which was altered without notice to, or knowledge or consent of, the insured, his representative, agent or broker.

(9) Failing, after payment of a claim, to inform insureds or beneficiaries, upon request by them, of the coverage under which payment has been made.

(10) Making known to insureds or claimants a practice of the insurer of appealing from arbitration awards in favor of insureds or claimants for the purpose of compelling them to accept settlements or compromises less than the amount awarded in arbitration.

(11) Delaying the investigation or payment of claims by requiring an insured, claimant, or the physician of either, to submit a preliminary claim report, and then requiring the subsequent submission of formal proof of loss forms, both of which submissions contain substantially the same information.

(12) Failing to settle claims promptly, where liability has become apparent, under one portion of the insurance policy coverage in order to influence settlement under other portions of the insurance policy coverage.

(13) Failing to provide promptly a reasonable explanation of the basis relied on in the insurance policy, in relation to

*the facts or applicable law, for the denial of a claim or for
the offer of a compromise settlement.*

*(14) Directly advising a claimant not to obtain the services
of an attorney.*

*(15) Misleading a claimant as to the applicable statute of
limitations.*

Fair Treatment

Another right that is ensured to the policyholder under his
or her policy with an insurance company is the right to fair
treatment. An insurance company is said to have a "fiduciary"
relationship with its customers. This means that the protection
of the policyholder's property is held in trust by the insurance
company, and therefore the company owes the policyholder
fair treatment. The insurance company is required to deal with
you fairly and cannot take advantage of your lack of knowledge
or deprive you of claim payments you are entitled to.

When an insurance company violates the fiduciary relationship with its customers and neglects to provide the protection
called for by the policy, the company can be seen to be acting
in "bad faith." In order for bad faith to exist, there must be
a conscious wrongdoing on the part of the company, and not
merely an honest mistake. As an illustration, if a company
were to deny a claim for an interior water leak caused by a
clogged rain gutter and cited the exclusion for drain backups,
it might be seen by a court to constitute an act of bad faith
for its misinterpretation of policy language. The company is
required to know that the exclusion being cited does not really
apply to such a loss. Denying your claim on the basis of this
exclusion is considered totally improper.

Bad faith has become the classic wolf's cry of attorneys and
policyholders who feel they have been improperly treated.
Claims of bad faith are routinely included in legal complaints

against insurance companies, whether well founded or not. The reason is that punitive damage awards for bad faith against insurance companies have risen to the multimillion dollar range. Many insurance people feel that this is a destructive trend that is also expensive to the insurance-buying public. The awards are paid out of premium dollars and the cost is passed on to the public via higher insurance costs.

Salvage

The insurance company has the right to take over the salvage of any kind of property as long as the policyholder has been compensated for its total value. If a house is damaged by fire, the company might salvage fixtures, appliances, and any other part of the building with remaining value as long as the policyholder has been paid for his or her total loss. Sometimes the insurance company will sell back the salvage goods to the policyholder and make a payment based on the value of the item less the value of the salvage. As an example, consider a broadloom wool carpet charred in a fire. Assume that the carpet is worth $3,000 undamaged, but that after the loss, it is worth $1,000. The insurance company might offer to pay the policyholder $2,000 based on the reduction in value of the carpet and allow the policyholder to keep the carpet. The policyholder is under no obligation to accept this offer and can insist on full payment for the carpet.

Most insurance companies do not directly involve themselves in the salvage process. They hire salvage companies that specialize in this kind of work. After a loss occurs, a salvage company will pick up damaged property and have it cleaned, repaired, and restored, and then sell it. It charges the insurance company for expenses incurred and adds a percentage for profit. The remaining money is paid to the insurance company as a return on the salvage operation.

There is another policy stipulation of which you should be informed when involved in a salvage situation.

The Standard Fire Policy states that "there can be no abandonment to this company of any property." This means that you cannot require the insurance company to take over possession of damaged property whether it retains salvage value or not. The prerogative rests with the insurance company to declare the property a total loss, and it can demand to take over the salvage, but you *cannot* demand that the company sell you the salvage, nor can you require it to take possession of the salvage. You always have the right to file a claim for a total loss, but you cannot require the company to pay your claim.

Statements

The policyholder has certain rights regarding claim statements. There are two kinds of statements that you may be asked to give in regard to a loss. The first is an informal statement, generally taken by the company representative at the time the loss is inspected. This kind of statement is usually handwritten by the adjuster or recorded on tape.

Informal statements are usually taken merely to record the facts surrounding a loss and to solidify a policyholder's story. Many companies require that a statement be taken on all theft claims regardless of magnitude or complexity. Just because a company representative wants to take a statement from you does not mean that something is wrong or that your claim is suspicious. It really is standard procedure in many cases. In the case of a questionable or complicated claim, a good adjuster will always attempt to get a statement from the policyholder. The existence of a statement will lessen the possibility that a policyholder's story will change over time.

An informal statement is not intended to limit a company's liability on a claim. If you were to file a burglary claim, for example, and report that a TV was the only item stolen, the company's liability would not be limited to the TV if you later discovered jewelry items taken as well. You might be reminded of the facts as recorded in the statement, but as long as there is a rational explanation for the inconsistency you should not have any trouble amending your claim.

There is no reason why it is inadvisable or contrary to your interest to give a representative an informal statement. It is merely an informal recording of facts. Remember, the statement is your story, your version of the facts, and as such it is also valuable to you. It will protect you to some extent and will also keep the company from altering the facts. It is important to keep in mind that there is *nothing* in the homeowners policy that requires a policyholder to provide the company with an informal statement.

The second kind of statement you may be asked to give is a formal statement under oath. This statement, in contrast to the informal statement, is required under a homeowners policy if requested by the company. In most every case, this formal or sworn statement is taken by an attorney and is in effect sworn court testimony. If you lie and the company can prove it, you are guilty of perjury. If you refuse to give a formal statement, it is a breach of the insurance contract and may render it void. Unlike an informal statement, sworn statements are generally required when the company feels that something is rotten in Denmark—when fraud is suspected. In some cases, a sworn statement is used as a scare tactic when fraud is suspected but cannot be proved. The hope is that the policyholder will withdraw the claim rather than commit perjury. In most cases, a company will have strong evidence of misconduct before a sworn statement is requested. The content of the formal statement can and will be used to convict you of fraud. It simply does not pay to misrepresent facts to an insurance company. If you are caught, your policy will be voided and your claim denied, or you will be prosecuted in court, or both.

Nonwaiver Agreements

An insurance company can sometimes forfeit its right to deny a claim merely by investigating the facts of the case. If a company leads a policyholder to believe that a claim will be paid or implies that it will be paid in some manner, the company may create what is known as an "estoppel" that prohibits it from denying the claim. This can hold true even though the investigation uncovers facts that clearly indicate that the claim is not covered.

In order to avoid waiving the right to deny a claim by conducting an investigation, many companies investigate questionable claims under a "nonwaiver agreement." This is a simple form that states that the company retains all of the rights provided it by the policy, including the right to deny the claim in question. By signing such an agreement, the policyholder states that he understands that the company is not committed to pay the claim just because the facts are being explored.

Reservation of Rights Letters

Another method that an insurance company has of protecting its right to deny a claim is the "reservation of rights letter." This letter is similar to a nonwaiver agreement, as it states that the company's investigation is being conducted with all rights reserved, including the right to deny the claim.

In the case of a questionable claim, a policyholder may be asked to sign a nonwaiver agreement at the onset of the investigation. If the insured refuses to sign the agreement—and he or she can—then a reservation of rights letter will usually be sent. At times a reservation of rights letter alone will be used, without an attempt being made to obtain a signed nonwaiver agreement. Most companies feel that a signed nonwaiver agreement is preferable to the mere sending of a reservation of rights letter as it places the company in a more advantageous position if it needs to deny the claim. If you sign a nonwaiver agreement, you are telling the company that you understand that the claim may be denied, and your signature on such a document may be seen as a mark of approval. A reservation of rights letter is merely a notice from the insurance company, without the implication of your agreement.

As a policyholder, you are under no obligation to sign a nonwaiver agreement, and can refuse to do so. In fact, signing the document does realistically weaken your position somewhat. Nonwaiver agreements and reservation of rights letters are used routinely, almost neurotically, by insurance companies whenever there is any potential for questions on a claim. In most cases these documents are totally irrelevant to the outcome of the claim.

Ultimately, the insurance company almost has to tell a policyholder outright that a claim is covered, go through the entire adjustment process, and then make a settlement offer before the right to deny the claim is waived. If the company does not go this far in indicating that a claim will be paid, it probably retains the right to denial, with or without a reservation of rights document. Any good adjuster knows this, and simply will not do anything to create an estoppel. In view of the moot nature of a nonwaiver agreement in most instances, it may be wise to go ahead and sign the document just to keep your relationship with the insurance company on a positive note.

The truth is that insurance companies have grown to be rather paranoid because of the liberal attitude of the courts toward policyholders. Insurance companies now feel that they must take every conceivable precaution to protect their rights and their interests. The investigation of claims under some form of reservation of rights document is standard operating procedure for most insurance companies, although these documents rarely alter the outcome of a claim or make any difference in the final decision of insurance companies or courts of law.

Cancellation

Policyholders have another important right to bear in mind. It concerns policy cancellation. A homeowners policy may be cancelled by the company or by the policyholder. If the company cancels, you will receive the full amount of unused premium payments on a pro rata basis. If you cancel, you receive slightly less than the remaining unused premium amount. The discrepancy in money refunded is attributed to the costs borne by the insurance company in writing the policy and in examining the risk. These expenses are the same regardless of the amount of time the policy is in effect.

As a policyholder, to cancel your policy you need only notify the company in writing of your desire to do so. The cancellation is effective the minute the company receives the notice as long as the request for cancellation is unconditional. You are also required to surrender your policy to the company and must do so at the time or shortly after your cancellation notice is delivered. At times, the company will not return the excess premium until the policy is surrendered.

If the company cancels, it is required to give five days' notice. This protects the policyholder, as the policyholder is the one faced with potential loss due to cancellation of a policy.

A specific insurance company's attitude toward cancellation will vary based upon the type of business that the company writes. A company writing business for a preferred class of customers may cancel a policy after only one or two claims are filed, especially if it experiences difficulty in settling the claim with the policyholder. Other companies will not cancel the policy until many claims have been filed. Many times, policyholders fear that filing property claims will increase their premiums. This is frequently the case with auto insurance, but it is generally not so with homeowners insurance. Typically, the rates for coverage will remain the same, and if a company feels that too many claims have been filed or that the policyholder is a bad risk, the policy will be cancelled or will not be renewed when the policy term expires. Fear of higher premiums or cancellation sometimes causes policyholders to avoid filing claims that are small or that might not be covered. It is important to keep in mind that if your insurance is cancelled, you will almost certainly be able to obtain comparative protection at a competitive price elsewhere without any trouble. Insurance is purchased to provide protection against loss, and when a loss is sustained, you should not be hesitant to take advantage of the protection you have paid for.

In Sum

When studying your rights, keep in mind:

- Policy interpretation is a difficult yet important aspect of insurance, and questions that come up in this area need to be carefully researched.
- The issue of third party negligence as a covered peril under homeowners policies is a significant development in insurance that indicates the changing nature of the field.
- Proximate cause and concurrent causation theory are two more principles that are undergoing changes, and will have a strong effect on the field of homeowners insurance in the future.
- Appraisal and suit are two avenues of recourse for dissatisfied policyholders.
- Subrogation is an aspect of insurance that is sometimes rele-

vant when claims are filed, and the informed policyholder
should be aware of the workings of this concept.

- Unfair Claim Settlement Practices Acts are laws that exist
  in most states regulating the activities of insurance companies
  on claims. Familiarize yourself with the law in your state.
- You are entitled to fair treatment from your insurance company, because of the nature of your relationship with the
  company.
- Salvage property is another issue that sometimes comes up
  in claim situations, and allows for creative alternatives in settling claims.
- There are two kinds of statements taken from policyholders
  by insurance companies, and you should be aware of the
  difference between them.
- Nonwaiver agreements are used by insurance companies to
  protect their rights. The homeowners policies do not require
  that the policyholder sign a nonwaiver agreement.
- An insurance policy can be cancelled by the company or by
  the policyholder. Be aware of your rights in the area of cancellation.

The most important thing to keep in mind about the subject
of homeowners insurance is that it does not have to be complicated, foreign, or difficult. With a minimum amount of study,
the typical homeowner can learn enough to effectively insure
his property and to pursue a claim through to a satisfactory
resolution. Another important point to remember is that technical knowledge is not necessary. An open, inquisitive attitude,
common sense, and a willingness to really address the questions
that come up in the area of homeowners insurance are all
more important than facts and information. It is hoped that
this book gives you a base of knowledge that makes you com-
fortable with the subject of homeowners insurance.

Index